Discipling A New Believer

Simple, Effective Basics

Larry Adams

Other Books by Larry Adams

Revelation: A Fresh Perspective
Did You Ever Realize…
Out On A Limb
That Your Prayers May Not Be Hindered
Future Focus

The Author may be contacted at LDA27019@gmail.com
Also, http://christiankontroversy.blogspot.com

Contents

foreword

In Matthew 28 Jesus tells us to go into all the world and make disciples of all peoples, baptizing them and teaching them to observe all that He has commanded us... Here we see at least what the beginning of discipleship is—Jesus defined "make disciples" as teaching then to observe all that he had commanded along with baptism. Simple, huh? It's amazing how people make things more complicated than need be. I've found over 70 items that Jesus commanded his disciples. Some of them are duplicates between Gospel accounts, some mean the same thing but are stated in a slightly different way, but there's a bunch of them.

One of the biggest issues facing the church in the US is that most Christians have never been formally discipled. This presents a problem for them in that they become afraid of sharing Jesus with others. If a person prays to receive Jesus, the one sharing Jesus does not know what to do with them except take them to church and hope the pastor can direct them. This book will greatly help in this issue. If you have never been formally discipled, simply take this book, read and study what is presented, and by the time you finish, you just might realize that the basic foundation of discipleship has been laid in your life. You can then take this book and use it to start the discipleship process in a new believer.

In John 11:38-44 we have the incident recorded of Lazarus being raised from death. After Jesus called Lazarus from the grave, He makes an interesting statement that ties directly into discipleship. Jesus stated in verse 44 after the description of Lazarus stumbling out of the grave still bound hand and foot by his grave clothes, "Unbind him."

When a person finds salvation in Jesus, they are still "bound hand and foot" in the grave clothes of the world they have just been resurrected from. Separation from God is death, whether now or when this body of ours expires. The new birth, in a very real sense is like being raised from death, being brought out of the grave of the world system that had been our total and only existence. (Galatian's 1:4) We need to be "unbound" from all the trappings of the world we had been existing in. Teaching a new believer all that Jesus has commanded us is the beginning of getting rid of all the grave clothes of the world we no longer need. At the beginning, a new Christian really has no practical understanding of the difference between their former life in the world and the new life in Christ. Teaching them to observe all that Jesus has commanded us is the first and simplest means of getting that difference across to the new Christian.

Many people suffer some form of trauma as young children. If the trauma is severe enough, the child will bury the event in their mind and conscience—that's the only means they have to cope with the intensity of the experience. That trauma will affect how they behave in certain situations as an adult. In 1 John 4:4 many people quote the last part out of context: "greater is he that is in you than he that is in the world." If you read the whole verse and the three before it, John identifies the context of that statement as the Christian overcoming the spirits of the Antichrist. That word in the Greek is translated some places as "overcome," and in others as "conquer." Both overcome and conquer require a confrontation, otherwise there will be no overcoming. God does not auto-magically go "abracadabra" and poof, the issue is gone. We must walk in faith into a confrontation with all the ways of the world we are bound by, all the suppressed traumas the world has us bound by, and pick them off one by one. God told the Israelites before they went into the promised land that He would not drive the people out ahead of time, because, if He did the wild beasts would multiply so fast that their presence would be worse than the battles they needed to fight against the people. God works in our lives event by event to bring us to maturity in Christ. Please don't try to circumvent God's ways.

There are five passages throughout Scripture that tell us that God wants us to pay attention to all His words, we do not have any permission or instruction from God to add to His words, nor to omit any of His words. Read Deuteronomy 4:2, 18:18-20; Proverbs 30:6, Jeremiah 26:2; Revelation 22:18-19. Personally, I call this God's curse on modifying His word. We are not greater than God, and we do not have any authority to choose which verses are true and not true. Treating verses as though they are not true is very effectively calling God a liar—not a good thing to do. You will find that the explanations provided in each chapter don't mince words. Many of the comments identify specifically what the difference is between the ways of the world and the ways of God, without toning down nor exaggerating the points that Scripture makes.

This book has 59 chapters identifying at least 75 items related to His commands. Each chapter discusses some of the items Jesus commanded us. There are several appendices which provide detailed studies of specific issues that will take a short time to read and study. The simplest way of using this book is to sit with the new believer once a week and go through a chapter or two or three. This could only take about 30-40 minutes at a time. Meeting a couple times a week would obviously get through the book faster - it really depends on the time available and the discipler and the disciplee. The appendices can be "assigned" as "homework" so that the disciplee can obtain deeper understanding on important issues. Be sure and bring your bibles with you when you discuss these things so you can look up any references that are included in a chapter. The disciplee's reading and studying of the word is an integral part of their growth.

The commands covered here fall into a few categories: our relation to God, our relation to others, and a category I call personal reflection, how we handle our thoughts and emotions regarding whatever the command might be. Identifying what relation each command applies to can be of great assistance in understanding how to apply the command to your life. Some of the beginning chapters have the specific label identified, others are not so identified and you will have to figure those out yourself. Get ready for one of the most important learning experiences of your Christian life

fear=Afraid

Matthew 10:28-31 (NASB) *"28 Do not fear those who kill the body but are unable to kill the soul; but rather fear Him who is able to destroy both soul and body in hell. 29 Are not two sparrows sold for a cent? And yet not one of them will fall to the ground apart from your Father. 30 But the very hairs of your head are all numbered. 31 So do not fear; you are more valuable than many sparrows."*

Luke 5:10 (NASB) *"10 and so also were James and John, sons of Zebedee, who were partners with Simon. And Jesus said to Simon, "Do not fear, from now on you will be catching men." "*

Luke 12:4-7 (NASB) *"4 "I say to you, My friends, do not be afraid of those who kill the body and after that have no more that they can do. 5 But I will warn you whom to fear: fear the One who, after He has killed, has authority to cast into hell; yes, I tell you, fear Him! 6 Are not five sparrows sold for two cents? Yet not one of them is forgotten before God. 7 Indeed, the very hairs of your head are all numbered. Do not fear; you are more valuable than many sparrows."*

Luke 21:9 (NASB) *"9 When you hear of wars and disturbances, do not be terrified; for these things must take place first, but the end does not follow immediately." "*

John 14:27 (NASB) *"27 Peace I leave with you; My peace I give to you; not as the world gives do I give to you. Do not let your heart be troubled, nor let it be fearful."*

Romans 8:15 (NASB) *'15 For you have not received a spirit of slavery leading to fear again, but you have received a spirit of adoption as sons by which we cry out, "Abba! Father!""*

1 Peter 3:14-15 (NASB) *"14 But even if you should suffer for the sake of righteousness, you are blessed. And do not fear their intimidation, and do not be troubled, 15 but sanctify Christ as Lord in your hearts, always being ready to make a defense to everyone who asks you to give an account for the hope that is in you, yet with gentleness and reverence;"*

Revelation 2:10 (NASB) "10 Do not fear what you are about to suffer. Behold, the devil is about to cast some of you into prison, so that you will be tested, and you will have tribulation for ten days. Be faithful until death, and I will give you the crown of life."

There are many things in life that can cause us to fear. Loss of a job, contracting a fatal disease, the death of a loved one, being a victim of a crime of any sort, war, these are just some of the things that can happen to us as we travel through life. In some parts the world today there is also the threat of death for being a Christian. The passages above identify situations such as death, job future and how to keep eating and protected, wars in various places in the world, persecution for being a Christian, and general suffering. Note also that God provides us with His assurance of being for us, His peace, His provision, His adoption of us as His children, so that we have assurance that we are not alone, but have Him at our side no matter what the situation may be.

Hebrews 10:30-31 talks about God being the one to take vengeance, we are not to do that. Those who need vengeance are warned that it is terrifying to fall into the hands of a living God. We need to keep focused on the assurance that those who are against God (or his children) will ultimately get God's vengeance, eternity in the lake of fire. Everyone is going to get what they desire and deserve in the end.

As Christians, we have eternity with God. The problems we suffer with here in this short (comparatively) time on Earth will be just a "blink of the eye" compared to eternity. God will work out everything in our favor - we just need to stay focused on what He wants of us.

Fear is an internal emotion that involves both our mind and heart. It can cause us to lash out at others or God, but it begins within us. Perfect love (God's love) casts out fear (1 John 4:18) (Personal Reflection)

Repent

Matthew 4:17 (NASB) "17 From that time Jesus began to preach and say, "Repent, for the kingdom of heaven is at hand." "

The word in the Greek that is translated "repent" simply means

"g3340. μετανοέω metanoeō; from 3326 and 3539; to change one's mind or purpose"

See the chapter "The New Birth" for a detailed study of the Scripture on "repent" and "believe."

Most people have a mindset that is based on the ways of the world and what is required to survive in that environment. God wants us to survive also, but the kingdom of heaven requires a different mindset. Romans 12:2 tells us that we need to be transformed by the renewing our mind—repent, a change of mind, is the basis for that transformation. We will be living in the eternal kingdom of heaven and here and now is where God wants us to become prepared for eternity.

Repent is the starting point of our salvation and takes place in our minds. (Personal Reflection)

Murder ⁊ Anger⁊ Derogatory Labeling

Matthew 5:22 (NASB) "22 But I say to you that everyone who is angry with his brother shall be guilty before the court; and whoever says to his brother, 'You good-for-nothing,' shall be guilty before the supreme court; and whoever says, 'You fool,' shall be guilty enough to go into the fiery hell."

In John 13:34-35 we find that Jesus wants us to love one another. (See chapter "Love One Another") The world thinks there is nothing wrong with using derogatory terms to describe people. Anger, in and of itself, is not wrong or sin, however, how we handle that anger is the point here. Other people, whether they know God or not, are created in His image, and we have no authority to murder one created in God's image or use such derogatory names against His image and likeness. We are to pray for those who persecute us, generally those who do something against or offensive to us (See chapters: "Give, Pray, Fast in Secret," and "Prayer"). Eph. 4:26 tells us to not let the sun go down on our anger. All of these things mentioned here pertain to our relation to others.

Reconcile Quickly

Matthew 5:23-24 (NASB) "23 Therefore if you are presenting your offering at the altar, and there remember that your brother has something against you, 24 leave your offering there before the altar and go; first be reconciled to your brother, and then come and present your offering."

The longer something bad drags out, the more Satan has an opportunity to get involved and make things worse. Bad attitudes between ourselves and someone else can and will interfere with our relation to God. Paul tells us that as much as possible to be at peace with others (Rom. 12:18). Two believers holding a grudge against each other is in obvious violation of Jesus command to love one another (See chapter: "Love One Another").

Adultery

Matthew 5:27-28 (NASB) "27 "You have heard that it was said, 'You shall not commit adultery'; 28 but I say to you that everyone who looks at a woman with lust for her has already committed adultery with her in his heart." "

Jesus here states that it is just as bad to harbor sin in your heart as it is to actually commit the physical act of sin. In 1 Samuel 16:7 we are told that man looks on the outside of a person, but God looks on the heart. Other people may not be aware of the sin we harbor in our heart, but God knows what that sin is. Adultery is what is in focus here in what Jesus states. The concept of sinning in our hearts applies to any and every sin. This issue falls under the category of Personal Reflection - what we do in our mind and heart.

Divorce

Matthew 5:31-32 (NASB) "31 "It was said, 'Whoever sends his wife away, let him give her A certificate of divorce'; 32 but I say to you that everyone who divorces his wife, except for the reason of unchastity, makes her commit adultery; and whoever marries a divorced woman commits adultery."

Sin always has consequences. In God's economy, isolation is one of the consequences of divorce. Mark 10:9 and Matthew 19:6 tells that what God has put together let not man take it apart. God instituted marriage, and the experiences of millions of couples shows that the weakness in our relation to God are brought out most poignantly in marriage. (See Malachi 2:16; Mark 10:2-12; Luke 16:18; Romans 7:2-3; 1 Corinthians 7:11-13; Matthew 19:8-9; Hebrews 13:4)

This issue emphasizes the importance of following God's still small voice in finding a marriage partner. We get ourselves in trouble by following our lusts instead of God's voice. We frequently act on our lusts and attempt to put it under "God's blessing." The problem with that is multi-fold. We put ourselves in a bind with God in by using His institution for our lusts, but that does not remove any obligation on us to obey His mandates. We put the name of God to shame by using His institution for our own lusts and them breaking His mandate by getting divorced because the lust does not last. Take your time and make sure you are following God's leading, not only in getting married, but in everything else you do.

Oaths

Matthew 5:33-37 (NASB) "33 "Again, you have heard that the ancients were told, 'You shall not make false vows, but shall fulfill your vows to the Lord.' 34 But I say to you, make no oath at all, either by heaven, for it is the throne of God, 35 or by the earth, for it is the footstool of His feet, or by Jerusalem, for it is the city of the great King. 36 Nor shall you make an oath by your head, for you cannot make one hair white or black. 37 But let your statement be, 'Yes, yes' or 'No, no'; anything beyond these is of evil."

This command is related to one of the Ten Commandments where we are told to not take God's name in vain. Most people in their thinking default to swear or cuss words as taking the mane of the Lord in vain. There is more to it than that. When you swear by God's name, or anything else, you are doing so in vain. Those things and people have nothing to do with what you are swearing nor does God tell you to do such things.

In Judges 11, we have the account of Jephthah who prayed to God for him to win a battle, and swore that when the victory was won and he came back home, he would sacrifice to God the first think that he saw come out of his house. It turned out that the battle was won, and his daughter was the first thing he saw come out of his house. God never promotes or condones the sacrifice of people to Himself. Jephthah did this all on his own—he swore to God that he would do this without any prompting from God to take that oath. Practically speaking, Jephthah was trying to talk God into giving him the victory and accepting payment from him. God does not work that way. Lesson learned?

Turn the Other Cheek

Matthew 5:38-41 (NASB) "38 "You have heard that it was said, 'AN eye for an eye, and A tooth for A tooth.' 39 But I say to you, do not resist an evil person; but whoever slaps you on your right cheek, turn the other to him also. 40 If anyone wants to sue you and take your shirt, let him have your coat also. 41 Whoever forces you to go one mile, go with him two."

Notice that this focuses on our relation to other people, not the Devil himself. We are to resist the Devil (James 4:7 in the context of submitting to God), but not people. Ephesians 6:10-18 tells us our battle is not against people, but evil forces in the heavenlies. Matthew 5:44 tells us to love our enemies and pray for those who persecute you. All these references are in the context of relating to other people. People need God's love and salvation, not a critical condemning attitude from a Christian. The situation behind going the extra mile is from the Roman army culture back in bible times. A soldier could conscript any of the local people to carry his pack for one mile. Jesus wants us to do better than the basic requirement.

Many years ago, a coworker's trailer caught fire and they lost everything. They decided to build a "real" house on the property (which they owned). I volunteered to help with the electrical and plumbing. I was the only one that stuck it out to the end and helped them move in. He knew I was a Christian before the fire happened. That testimony of staying beside him though he entire effort meant something to him. I could have "dropped out" part way through, or just done the minimum required, but he got a first-class job that passed all the inspections the first time. That's what it means to "go the extra mile."

Borrowers

Matthew 5:42 (NASB) "42 Give to him who asks of you, and do not turn away from him who wants to borrow from you."

The things we have, our possessions are not to be worshiped as idols in our life. Acts 2:42-45 tells us that the new believers shared their possessions as any had need. There is a difference between "need" and "want." We are not to be an enabler of anyone's envy of another's possessions (a form of idolatry) "

Whatever we have, we need to be good stewards of those things, but there needs to be a clarification of who owns what. We may pay money for something, and according to the world system, we own it. In God's scheme of things, He is the owner of everything, we are just His servants taking care of it, we are not going to take it with us when we die, there will be no need of it in heaven. So, if there is a need in someone else's life, and we have the means to take care of that need, we should do it. To the one who knows to do right and doesn't do it, to him it is sin. (James 4:17) Jesus told a parable in Luke 11:5-8 of a friend who was asked in the middle of the night for bread because a traveler arrived. The one asking for bread was persistent, and the friend relented and gave all that was needed. Helping each other when there are real needs is another way of demonstrating our love for each other. (See chapter, "Love One Another.")

Pray for Your Persecutors

Matthew 5:43-48 (NASB) "43 "You have heard that it was said, 'You shall love your neighbor and hate your enemy.' 44 But I say to you, love your enemies and pray for those who persecute you, 45 so that you may be sons of your Father who is in heaven; for He causes His sun to rise on the evil and the good, and sends rain on the righteous and the unrighteous. 46 For if you love those who love you, what reward do you have? Do not even the tax collectors do the same? 47 If you greet only your brothers, what more are you doing than others? Do not even the Gentiles do the same? 48 Therefore you are to be perfect, as your heavenly Father is perfect."

Going beyond the normal or typical is identified again in the specifics Jesus presents here. These issues include legal problems. In going beyond the typical ways of the world, we become more and more like our heavenly father who blesses both the righteous and unrighteous with sunshine and rain. It is when we go "above and beyond the call of duty" that we qualify for rewards from God. God is beyond reproach in his giving basic blessings. What we do with the things God gives us makes the difference. (See "Appendix A: Using what God gives us")

Give, Pray, Fast in Secret

Matthew 6:1-6 (NASB) "1 "Beware of practicing your righteousness before men to be noticed by them; otherwise you have no reward with your Father who is in heaven. 2 "So when you give to the poor, do not sound a trumpet before you, as the hypocrites do in the synagogues and in the streets, so that they may be honored by men. Truly I say to you, they have their reward in full. 3 But when you give to the poor, do not let your left hand know what your right hand is doing, 4 so that your giving will be in secret; and your Father who sees what is done in secret will reward you. 5 "When you pray, you are not to be like the hypocrites; for they love to stand and pray in the synagogues and on the street corners so that they may be seen by men. Truly I say to you, they have their reward in full. 6 But you, when you pray, go into your inner room, close your door and pray to your Father who is in secret, and your Father who sees what is done in secret will reward you."

Being a "show-off" or bragging about how much you give or pray, only gives you the reward of praise from other people, nothing from God. The rewards from God are eternal, rewards from other people are only temporary. Put your efforts into what gives the greatest reward. That requires humility before both God and other people. That does not mean you are prohibited from attending a "prayer" meeting at your local congregation — Scripture does tell us to pray for one another (James 5:16; Ephesians 6:18; 1 Timothy 2:1). Mark 1:35 and Luke 5:16 are examples of Jesus going off by himself to pray. These verses are used as a basis for "quiet time." A time of solitude where you can pray and/or read the bible for your own spiritual growth. You also need the fellowship of others and to sit under a good bible teacher in your local congregation. There will be things you learn in the public forum and other things you will learn in the private forum. You need both. Every other Christian you participate with in the public forum should be in the process of growing spiritually just as you are. God does not "play favorites" with his children—they are all precious to Him. Chances are, the things you learn in private are things others have also learned if they are older Christians than you. Bragging is simply seeking the approval of other people instead of God. God will reward you for maintaining that personal private relation to Him. Don't snub Him.

Vain Repetition

Matthew 6:7-8 (NASB) "7 "And when you are praying, do not use meaningless repetition as the Gentiles do, for they suppose that they will be heard for their many words. 8 So do not be like them; for your Father knows what you need before you ask Him."

God is intelligent, He knows what you are needing. The reference to "Gentiles" in this verse simply identifies the type of gods they worshiped — wood, stone, metal, etc., which really do not exist and have no means of hearing to begin with. If God can see the end from the beginning (Isaiah 46:10), He already knows what your real needs are. We pray, not to inform God of something he does not already know, but to stay humble before Him and to participate in what He wants to accomplish in our lives.

In the prayer example most frequently referred to as "The Lord's Prayer" in Matthew 6:9-13, Jesus identified some very simple aspects of what prayer should be. First is the identification of God the Father in heaven, and that He is holy. Second is a statement of confirmation that He will be (and already is) the victor in all aspects both in heaven and earth. Third is a simple request for our sustenance for each day. Fourth is a request for forgiveness of our sins, in the same manner as we forgive those who sin against us. Fifth, is a request that may seem a bit confusing at first. The translation of this part of the prayer is based on the Old English of the King James Version In our current dialect of English, it simply means do not let us fall into the evil results of temptation—we are going to encounter temptation from Satan and his world system, but we don't need to "go the distance" with it and suffer the evil results those temptations would lead to. This is a request for the strength, insight and courage to identify the temptation and just simply say "No!" and walk away.

There is no requirement to only mimic these specific words, although there is no harm in doing so. The real point is to include in your prayers, the praise due God, a humble submission to Him so that His victory would be evident in us, His meeting of our real needs, forgiveness of our sins, and the wisdom in each situation we encounter for how to handle it His way. This could take anywhere from 5 minutes to an hour or more depending on how many situations are going on in our lives at the time. It is not the length or shortness of the prayer, it is the content that counts.

Worry

Matthew 6:25-34 (NASB) "25 "For this reason I say to you, do not be worried about your life, as to what you will eat or what you will drink; nor for your body, as to what you will put on. Is not life more than food, and the body more than clothing? 26 Look at the birds of the air, that they do not sow, nor reap nor gather into barns, and yet your heavenly Father feeds them. Are you not worth much more than they? 27 And who of you by being worried can add a single hour to his life? 28 And why are you worried about clothing? Observe how the lilies of the field grow; they do not toil nor do they spin, 29 yet I say to you that not even Solomon in all his glory clothed himself like one of these. 30 But if God so clothes the grass of the field, which is alive today and tomorrow is thrown into the furnace, will He not much more clothe you? You of little faith! 31 Do not worry then, saying, 'What will we eat?' or 'What will we drink?' or 'What will we wear for clothing?' 32 For the Gentiles eagerly seek all these things; for your heavenly Father knows that you need all these things. 33 But seek first His kingdom and His righteousness, and all these things will be added to you.34 "So do not worry about tomorrow; for tomorrow will care for itself. Each day has enough trouble of its own."

Luke 6:38 (NASB) "38 Give, and it will be given to you. They will pour into your lap a good measure—pressed down, shaken together, and running over. For by your standard of measure it will be measured to you in return." "

"Why pray when you can worry?" That's not the way God works things, even though the world may think that way. God is more concerned with you than you can imagine. He has set things in such a way that the animals of the field and air, and the foliage are taken care of and are beautiful. He cares for you even more, so why would we even think for a moment that He would not treat us at least as well. The corresponding principle is that if we hoard the basics we need, the supply will dry up. All we have as far as clothing, food, etc., is from God, and is to be used not only for ourselves, but for others also. In Acts, we read about the early church in chapters 3 and 4. They sold what they had and made sure that those in need were provided for. God can miraculously provide, or work through others to meet the need for whatever the situation may be. In either case, He provides.

Judging

Matthew 7:1-5 (NASB) "1 "Do not judge so that you will not be judged. 2 For in the way you judge, you will be judged; and by your standard of measure, it will be measured to you. 3 Why do you look at the speck that is in your brother's eye, but do not notice the log that is in your own eye? 4 Or how can you say to your brother, 'Let me take the speck out of your eye,' and behold, the log is in your own eye? 5 You hypocrite, first take the log out of your own eye, and then you will see clearly to take the speck out of your brother's eye."

Luke 6:37-38 (NASB) "37 "Do not judge, and you will not be judged; and do not condemn, and you will not be condemned; pardon, and you will be pardoned. 38 Give, and it will be given to you. They will pour into your lap a good measure—pressed down, shaken together, and running over. For by your standard of measure it will be measured to you in return." "

It seems that God does not totally pre-establish all the standards we will be judged by — He leaves some of that up to us. In Revelation 20:12 tells us that our rewards are based on what we do. 2 Corinthians 5:10 tells us that each Christian will appear before Christ to be rewarded for the things they do, either good or bad. Romans 2:5-6 tells us that in the end God will judge based on what we do. None of us are without sin. We wrestle with it each and every day. We need to focus on ourselves more than others who are also wrestling with sin each and every day. The sins we harbor in our hearts may be worse than the ones we expose in others—we may be exposing those to help hide our own.

Instead of focusing on pointing out sins, we need to be generous in our giving. Not just money, but forgiveness, time, effort, transportation, whatever God has given us. 1 Peter 4:8 tells us that love covers a multitude of sins. Give love in whatever practical means available and you just might not have the time to pick out other's sins.

Pearls Before Swine

Matthew 7:6 (NASB) "6 "Do not give what is holy to dogs, and do not throw your pearls before swine, or they will trample them under their feet, and turn and tear you to pieces."

I've phrased this as "If you cast your pearls before swine, they'll drag you through their mud." I can't tell you how many people I have personally known who have disobeyed this command and suffered greatly both emotionally and financially. There are those among us who only have contempt and evil in regards to anything that is holy or righteous or godly. It is not that we simply write them off and let them go to hell, but we need to pray for them that God would use someone to get through to them so they would be more open to hearing and considering the Gospel.

Seek the Holy Spirit

Matthew 7:7-11 (NASB) "7 "Ask, and it will be given to you; seek, and you will find; knock, and it will be opened to you. 8 For everyone who asks receives, and he who seeks finds, and to him who knocks it will be opened. 9 Or what man is there among you who, when his son asks for a loaf, will give him a stone? 10 Or if he asks for a fish, he will not give him a snake, will he? 11 If you then, being evil, know how to give good gifts to your children, how much more will your Father who is in heaven give what is good to those who ask Him!"

Luke 11:9-13 (NASB) "9 "So I say to you, ask, and it will be given to you; seek, and you will find; knock, and it will be opened to you. 10 For everyone who asks, receives; and he who seeks, finds; and to him who knocks, it will be opened. 11 Now suppose one of you fathers is asked by his son for a fish; he will not give him a snake instead of a fish, will he? 12 Or if he is asked for an egg, he will not give him a scorpion, will he? 13 If you then, being evil, know how to give good gifts to your children, how much more will your heavenly Father give the Holy Spirit to those who ask Him?""

The general principle here is found in the Greek for "ask," "seek," and "knock." The Greek indicates these are a continuing process, i.e., keep on asking, keep on seeking, keep on knocking. The earthly comparison is that of a father giving good things to his son, and God considers us His children, He is going to give at least like an earthly father, but even more. What is given is whatever good thing God deems appropriate at the time, including the Holy Spirit.

Scholars are divided on what the "giving of the Holy Spirit" really means. Many think this is a reference to what would become known as the "Day of Pentecost," when the Holy Spirit fell on the disciples in power. Others modify the sense of the words to mean we need to ask for salvation. The problem with the second idea is that there are no instances or examples of a sinner's prayer (or prayer of salvation) in the bible. Everywhere that someone found salvation, the only description given is that they believed. That's not to say God does not honor such a prayer. Many times, that prayer brings a person to a situation where they do believe. It is the believing that makes the difference between salvation and not having it, not how one arrives at that belief.

The significant point here is that it is not just a matter of a flippant request to God and no more need to bring it up again. Keeping on with the asking, seeking, knocking, keeps us in a humble relation to God, and keeps us focused on participating with God in what He is doing in our lives. All too often we pray for a situation thinking someone else needs God's touch and it turns out that God touches us instead. We need the power of the Holy Spirit not only to be able to preach the gospel boldly, and to endure persecution, but we need the power of the Holy Spirit to be persistent in whatever the Lord leads in our lives.

False Prophets

Matthew 7:15-20 (NASB) "15 "Beware of the false prophets, who come to you in sheep's clothing, but inwardly are ravenous wolves. 16 You will know them by their fruits. Grapes are not gathered from thorn bushes nor figs from thistles, are they? 17 So every good tree bears good fruit, but the bad tree bears bad fruit. 18 A good tree cannot produce bad fruit, nor can a bad tree produce good fruit. 19 Every tree that does not bear good fruit is cut down and thrown into the fire. 20 So then, you will know them by their fruits."

Matt 24:11, 24; Mark 13:22; Luke 6:26; Acts 13:6; 2 Pet 2:1; 1 John 4:1; Rev 16:13; 19:20; 20:10 all are references to the danger of false prophets. False prophets are those who proclaim something that sounds like it might be good, but is not inspired by God, might contain some phrases that are true, but generally is something false and deceptive. The proof of a good or bad prophet is simply the fruit of their life, and does what they prophesy actually come to be. They can be good word smiths, but it is not just the content of what they say, Satan will use phrases of truth in his deceptive tactics just to make the deception harder to expose. False prophets, will always have something about their behavior that is not godly. In Acts 17, the Berean's listened to Paul, then went to the Scriptures to verify what he had said. We need to do that with everyone we listen to regarding the bible, no matter what kind of credentials they may have. And we need to examine the Scriptures for more than, "Yes, that word is used in that verse." We need to evaluate the context to make certain that the wording preached is not twisted out of context and given an unusual definition that does not fit with what is written. We need to remember that even preachers are only people who also have to deal with sin on a daily basis. Sometimes they can be wrong, hopefully rarely, but it can happen.

Persecution, Cares of the World

Matthew 13:1-30 (NASB) "1 That day Jesus went out of the house and was sitting by the sea. 2 And large crowds gathered to Him, so He got into a boat and sat down, and the whole crowd was standing on the beach. 3 And He spoke many things to them in parables, saying, "Behold, the sower went out to sow; 4 and as he sowed, some seeds fell beside the road, and the birds came and ate them up. 5 Others fell on the rocky places, where they did not have much soil; and immediately they sprang up, because they had no depth of soil. 6 But when the sun had risen, they were scorched; and because they had no root, they withered away. 7 Others fell among the thorns, and the thorns came up and choked them out. 8 And others fell on the good soil and *yielded a crop, some a hundredfold, some sixty, and some thirty. 9 He who has ears, let him hear." 18 "Hear then the parable of the sower. 19 When anyone hears the word of the kingdom and does not understand it, the evil one comes and snatches away what has been sown in his heart. This is the one on whom seed was sown beside the road. 20 The one on whom seed was sown on the rocky places, this is the man who hears the word and immediately receives it with joy; 21 yet he has no firm root in himself, but is only temporary, and when affliction or persecution arises because of the word, immediately he falls away. 22 And the one on whom seed was sown among the thorns, this is the man who hears the word, and the worry of the world and the deceitfulness of wealth choke the word, and it becomes unfruitful. 23 And the one on whom seed was sown on the good soil, this is the man who hears the word and understands it; who indeed bears fruit and brings forth, some a hundredfold, some sixty, and some thirty." 24 Jesus presented another parable to them, saying, "The *kingdom of heaven may be compared to a man who sowed good seed in his field. 25 But while his men were sleeping, his enemy came and sowed tares among the wheat, and went away. 26 But when the wheat sprouted and bore grain, then the tares became evident also. 27 The slaves of the landowner came and said to him, 'Sir, did you not sow good seed in your field? How then does it have tares?' 28 And he said to them, 'An enemy has done this!' The slaves *said to him, 'Do you want us, then, to go and gather them up?' 29 But he *said, 'No; for while you are gathering up the tares, you may uproot the wheat with them. 30 Allow both to grow together until the harvest; and in the time of the harvest I will say to the reapers, "First gather up the tares and bind them in bundles to burn them up; but gather the wheat into my barn."'"*

Let's start with the most pertinent to us—the second and third soil types where seed was sown. The second type never developed any depth of root and therefore ran away when persecution took place. The third type took root, but did not tolerate the weeds and thistles, the cares and difficulties of life and turned to the false security in wealth. Sticking with the spiritual growth process takes focus and concentration and effort on our part. (See "Appendix C: Completing the work Christ gives us")

We happen to be in a spiritual war, the Devil against us. If he cannot keep us from becoming a Christian, he definitely wants to keep us from becoming an effective Christian. According to the enemy, it's OK to attend church services, but not OK to witness or testify to others what Jesus has done in our lives. Persecution, cares and worries of life, and the temptation of money are used against us to distract and dissuade us from being what God wants us to be and do.

What Jesus wants from us, according to this parable, is to find the good soil (verse 23), good spiritual nutrition and grow in faith. He wants us to be able to stand up to persecution, any usual worldly messes and troubles, and the distraction to get more money so we don't have to depend on God's provision. It does not happen overnight. Baby's take around 18 years to grow up, the spiritual corollary might take almost as long. Small children want to do big people things long before they are old enough and strong enough to accomplish them. We find the same temptation in spiritual matters. We need patience to see things through God's way, not the way of the flesh or the world.

God is not going to auto-magically take away the situations of the world we live in so we live a problem free life. We will have to face difficulties, some worse than others. Jesus told us that we are to be in the world, but not of the world (summarized from John 15:19 and 17:14-16). In some sentence structures, the word "of" can be used to indicate "source." We physically must exist on this planet, but our source of direction, sustenance, motivation, goals, etc., are not to be worldly, but godly.

Give everything for the kingdom of heaven

Matthew 13:31-52 (NASB) "31 He presented another parable to them, saying, "The kingdom of heaven is like a mustard seed, which a man took and sowed in his field; 32 and this is smaller than all other seeds, but when it is full grown, it is larger than the garden plants and becomes a tree, so that the birds of the air come and nest in its branches." 33 He spoke another parable to them, "The kingdom of heaven is like leaven, which a woman took and hid in three pecks of flour until it was all leavened." 34 All these things Jesus spoke to the crowds in parables, and He did not speak to them without a parable. 35 This was to fulfill what was spoken through the prophet: "I will open MY mouth in parables; I will utter things hidden since the foundation of the world." 36 Then He left the crowds and went into the house. And His disciples came to Him and said, "Explain to us the parable of the tares of the field." 37 And He said, "The one who sows the good seed is the Son of Man, 38 and the field is the world; and as for the good seed, these are the sons of the kingdom; and the tares are the sons of the evil one; 39 and the enemy who sowed them is the devil, and the harvest is the end of the age; and the reapers are angels. 40 So just as the tares are gathered up and burned with fire, so shall it be at the end of the age. 41 The Son of Man will send forth His angels, and they will gather out of His kingdom all stumbling blocks, and those who commit lawlessness, 42 and will throw them into the furnace of fire; in that place there will be weeping and gnashing of teeth. 43 Then the righteous will shine forth as the sun in the kingdom of their Father. He who has ears, let him hear. 44 "The kingdom of heaven is like a treasure hidden in the field, which a man found and hid again; and from joy over it he goes and sells all that he has and buys that field. 45 "Again, *the kingdom of heaven is like a merchant seeking fine pearls, 46 and upon finding one pearl of great value, he went and sold all that he had and bought it. 47 "Again, the kingdom of heaven is like a dragnet cast into the sea, and gathering fish of every kind; 48 and when it was filled, they drew it up on the beach; and they sat down and gathered the good fish into containers, but the bad they threw away. 49 So it will be at the end of the age; the angels will come forth and take out the wicked from among the righteous, 50 and will throw them into the furnace of fire; in that place there will be weeping and gnashing of teeth. 51 "Have you understood all these things?" They *said to Him, "Yes." 52 And Jesus said to them, "Therefore every scribe who has become a disciple of the kingdom of heaven is like a head of a household, who brings out of his treasure things new and old." "*

Most of the commands Christ gives us are really obvious things that contain words such as "No," or "Don't," or "avoid," or something of that nature. Here in these parables we find it a little different. These parables give us word pictures of what it takes, and what He wants of us, as it pertains to the kingdom of heaven.

What is a "kingdom?" That is a place and situation where there is a great ruler who has power to make things happen, and there are citizens of that kingdom who willingly follow that ruler. We are the citizens of the kingdom of heaven (kingdom of God is used in another gospel and means the same thing). God is the great ruler of this kingdom. We become citizens of this kingdom by believing on Jesus as the only means of finding forgiveness for our sins because He shed His blood on the cross, paying the penalty for our sins (Romans 6:23), and then being resurrected from death. We become part of God's family and kingdom at the same time.

The first two and fifth parables quoted here indicate how extensive the kingdom of heaven will become—God wants us to be part of all that. The others indicate how precious that kingdom is, and that it is worth sacrificing everything we have to be part of that kingdom. We need to be wary of letting other things distract us, nothing else comes even close to the value of what we have as children of God. (See the previous chapter, "Persecution, Cares of the World" the second and third seed/soil types.)

Traditions

Matthew 15:1-11 (NASB) "1 Then some Pharisees and scribes *came to Jesus from Jerusalem and said, 2 "Why do Your disciples break the tradition of the elders? For they do not wash their hands when they eat bread." 3 And He answered and said to them, "Why do you yourselves transgress the commandment of God for the sake of your tradition? 4 For God said, 'Honor your father and mother,' and, 'HE who speaks evil of father or mother is to be put to death.' 5 But you say, 'Whoever says to his father or mother, "Whatever I have that would help you has been given to God," 6 he is not to honor his father or his mother.' And by this you invalidated the word of God for the sake of your tradition. 7 You hypocrites, rightly did Isaiah prophesy of you: 8 'This people honors ME with their lips, But their heart is far away from ME. 9 'But in vain do they worship ME, Teaching as doctrines the precepts of men.'" 10 After Jesus called the crowd to Him, He said to them, "Hear and understand. 11 It is not what enters into the mouth that defiles the man, but what proceeds out of the mouth, this defiles the man.""

The very first question asked of Jesus in this encounter reveals what was really important to the Pharisees—traditions. The response given by Jesus points out that those traditions were in violation of God's commandments. It is really easy to try to put the things of God into rules and regulations, or traditions, "We've always done it that way!" We are to walk by faith, not by sight, as the Apostle Paul wrote in 2 Corinthians 5:7.

That involves being able to listen to the "still small voice of the Lord," among other things. That still small voice is way down deep in our spirit, not a "booming voice" in our heads. It is easy to ignore that voice. John 10:27 tells us that Jesus' sheep hear his voice. The requirement for listening to His voice, has existed since Adam and Eve. Deuteronomy 28 tells us that if we listen to the voice of the Lord, there are certain blessings. Verse 15 states that if we do not listen to the voice of the Lord, there are curses involved. There are at least three times as many verses regarding the curses as there are the blessings. That should show us just how important listening to the voice of the Lord really is.

The traditions of the Pharisees manipulated things so that they could "legally" circumvent the legitimate commands of God, like the Ten Commandments in Exodus 20— "legally" according to their twisted traditions. This is brought out in Jesus descriptions quoted from Isaiah.

Jesus sums up things to the crowd by identifying that what is in the heart of the Pharisees, and people in general, is what makes them defiled from God's perspective. (Matthew 15:11-20; Mark 7:15-23) Jeremiah 17:9 tells us that the heart is deceitful and desperately wicked. That is something God wants to change in us—be willing to let Him work that in us.

Evil Thoughts

Matthew 15:16-19 (NASB) "16 Jesus said, "Are you still lacking in understanding also? 17 Do you not understand that everything that goes into the mouth passes into the stomach, and is eliminated? 18 But the things that proceed out of the mouth come from the heart, and those defile the man. 19 For out of the heart come evil thoughts, murders, adulteries, fornications, thefts, false witness, slanders."

The evil things mentioned here mostly relate to what we do with and toward other people. The contrast to these evil things is found in: 1 Cor. 1:8; Eph. 1:4, 5:27; Phil. 1:10, 2:15; Col. 1:22; 2 Pet. 3:14; Jude 1:24; Rev. 14:5. These are references to the way God wants us to be, blameless. Blameless means that you cannot be accused of anything wrong. Obviously, the list of things in verse 19 are all wrong things. We must have a change of heart and mind. See "Appendix B: The New Birth" for a detailed analysis of Scripture describing what goes on in the mind and heart of a person when finding salvation in Jesus. That change of heart doesn't happen like turning an electric light bulb on or off. It takes time to get unbound from the grave clothes of the world we are resurrected from. We cannot make that kind of change in our own strength. Matthew 18:3 tells us that we must be converted and become like children to enter the kingdom of heaven. That conversion is described in Appendix B referenced above. This is something done by the Holy Spirit, not by our own fleshy strength.

Causing Others to Sin

Matthew 18:4-6 (NASB) "4 Whoever then humbles himself as this child, he is the greatest in the kingdom of heaven. 5 And whoever receives one such child in My name receives Me; 6 but whoever causes one of these little ones who believe in Me to stumble, it would be better for him to have a heavy millstone hung around his neck, and to be drowned in the depth of the sea."

These verses are a continuation from the previous chapter titled "Evil Thoughts." Paul in 1 Corinthians 3:2, and the writer of Hebrews 5:12 both identify a problem that can afflict Christians—lack of spiritual growth, remaining spiritual infants instead of growing to maturity. Remaining a spiritual infant can stem from many causes, the person themselves, or others who's false teaching fails to include the truth of the whole Scripture. See "Appendix A: Using what God gives us" for a description of what God wants to accomplish in us. Part of that does include effort on our part.

Jesus describes how severe the judgment will be for anyone who causes a little child (physically or spiritually) to stumble and not be able to fulfill what God wants to do in their life. We don't have any right, authority, or instruction from God to pick and choose what parts of the bible are true and to be obeyed and ignore other parts. That act of ignoring other parts treats them as being not true, which is equivalent to calling God a liar. Acts 20:27 tells us that Paul, speaking to the elders from Ephesus, had not shrunk from declaring to them the whole counsel of God.

We need everything from God and His word in order to grow—that takes time and we need to stay humble and childlike, focused on God's goals in our lives.

forgive how Much?

Matthew 18:21-22 (NASB) "21 Then Peter came and said to Him, "Lord, how often shall my brother sin against me and I forgive him? Up to seven times?" 22 Jesus *said to him, "I do not say to you, up to seven times, but up to seventy times seven."

In Matthew 7:2 Jesus tells us that by the standard of measure we judge others, that will be the same standard God judges us by. If we want to be forgiven, we must forgive others, even if they continually keep sinning against us. After all, how many times in our Christian walk with God do we screw up and sin against Him?

Let's put some numbers to this. If you live to age 75, and only sin three times a day, that is 82,125 sins—each of which requires the death penalty… Seven times a day is 191, 625 sins—each requiring the death penalty… How many times do you want to die, or have anyone die? And eternity becomes that much longer… Each of us will be forgiven according to if and how we forgive others… (from the Lord's Prayer). See "Appendix D: Forgive" for more details of this issue.

Honor Parents

Matthew 19:19 (NASB) "19 Honor your father and mother; and You shall love your neighbor as yourself." "

This is a carry-over from the Old Testament. However, these verses illustrate a principle we need to pay attention to. Our love for parents will be mimicked in our love for God. Our love for God will be mimicked in our love for our parents. If you think in terms of "horizontal" and "vertical," both directions should be of the same caliber of love for others and God. 1 John 4:20-21 tells us that we cannot hate our brother and love God. It just does not work that way. The same goes for forgiveness, Matthew 6:15 tells us that if we do not forgive others for their sins against us, then neither will the Father forgive ours. This points out that the relationship between others, ourselves, and God works bidirectionally in both horizontal and vertical directions. You are God's gift to your parents for God's glory. Even if you do not think they did a good job of parenting, the presence of God's love in you must be witnessed to by how you honor your parents.

Your neighbor needs salvation in Jesus just as much as you do. Your love of God in your heart needs to be shown to other people. The word neighbor should not be restricted to those who live in a house next door to your own house. It should include everyone in the community of people who you interact with socially, commercially, or industrially. James 2:8 and Ephesians 5:29 are two verses (among others) which reiterate this principle. There is a difference between self-love and self-worship, the love aspect is what's important. We are to love our neighbor as we love ourselves, but only worship God. Honoring our parents should simply be an expression of our love for God and them.

Romans 15:4 tells us that what was written before, meaning the Old Testament, was written for our instruction and to give us hope. The Old Testament is very important to us so we can understand who God is, and His ways. The Old Testament (covenant) is the foundation for the New Testament (covenant).

Love God with All Your Heart

Matthew 22:37-40 (NASB) "37 And He said to him, "'You shall love the Lord your God with all your heart, and with all your soul, and with all your mind.' 38 This is the great and foremost commandment. 39 The second is like it, 'You shall love your neighbor as yourself.' 40 On these two commandments depend the whole Law and the Prophets." "

In Mark 12:30 and Luke 10:27 the word "strength" is added to the three basic "heart," "mind," and "soul." Most of the time when the Greek word "soul" is translated it refers to the entire entity of the person, not just a sub-part of the person. A few times, less than a handful, the word "soul" is used as a pseudonym for "spirit." In the Greek, the word for "spirit" is always translated "spirit," never "soul", and should apply the other way around. So, we have three parts to us, mind, heart, and spirit, based on the most consistent use of the words.

Some think man is only two-part until we find salvation in Jesus—body and soul. That is refuted very simply with the situation in Luke chapter 8, particularly verse 55 - a young girl had just been raised from death, and Luke records that "her spirit returned to her." Nothing can "return" to someplace if it had never been there before. To think otherwise is to make the meaning of all words idiocy and nonsense. And this was before Jesus resurrection, and the new birth did not exist until Jesus was resurrected. Jesus was the first with the new life, and the disciples were the next recipients the evening of His resurrection (John 20:22).

The basic point of this passage is that we are to devote every part of us to loving God. The result of that love of God is the love of our neighbor (See previous chapter titled "Honor Parents" for more details). Jesus also makes the point that the entire Law and Prophets (basically the Old Testament) are based on this bidirectional love.

Obey Authority

Matthew 23:1-3 (NASB) "1 Then Jesus spoke to the crowds and to His disciples, 2 saying: "The scribes and the Pharisees have seated themselves in the chair of Moses; 3 therefore all that they tell you, do and observe, but do not do according to their deeds; for they say things and do not do them."

Obey the law, but don't do the evil things the authorities do, thinking that they are above the law and it does not apply to them. The modern version of this is, "Do as I say, not as I do." That can be very difficult, no one is saying it is easy. We are not to live a contradictory life, God is not a God of confusion (1 Corinthians 14:33), and we are supposed to imitate Him.

Hebrews 13:7 and 3 John 1:11 tell us that there are those who's example we can and should imitate. These are godly people who imitate God. One of the goals of growing in spiritual maturity is to become one of those examples to other believers.

Beware the Abomination of Desolation

Matthew 24:15-21 (NASB) "15 "Therefore when you see the abomination of desolation which was spoken of through Daniel the prophet, standing in the holy place (let the reader understand), 16 then those who are in Judea must flee to the mountains. 17 Whoever is on the housetop must not go down to get the things out that are in his house. 18 Whoever is in the field must not turn back to get his cloak. 19 But woe to those who are pregnant and to those who are nursing babies in those days! 20 But pray that your flight will not be in the winter, or on a Sabbath. 21 For then there will be a great tribulation, such as has not occurred since the beginning of the world until now, nor ever will."

This admonition of Jesus points to what is popularly called the "End Times." There is some controversy about this, some think it was fulfilled by Antiochus Epiphanies around 168BC. There are some major differences between Daniel's description and exactly what Antiochus actually did. What he did was not a perfect match to Daniel's vision, even though, in general, what Antiochus did was abominable, downright terrible. The other thing to note is that Jesus did NOT say, "When you saw the abomination…" Jesus made this statement approximately 190 years after Antiochus did his thing. One would think that Jesus being fully God and fully Man, He would have known better, if Antiochus had already fulfilled this. The use of the word "when" indicates that the event is yet to happen in the future whether near future or far distant future. This is simply based on when the statement was made and paying attention to the words actually written. Jesus indicates that whatever this Abomination is, it has not yet happened, thereby lending credibility to the reality of the book of Daniel.

If you happen to be in Israel during the End Times, take heed of this.

Jesus Will Return

Matthew 26:64 (NASB) "64 Jesus said to him, "You have said it yourself; nevertheless I tell you, hereafter you will see the Son of Man sitting at the right hand of Power, and coming on the clouds of heaven." "

Psalms 110:1 and Mark 14:62 also refer to the Son of Man seated at the right hand of God, and coming again. Acts 1:9-11 records for us some angels speaking to the disciples who just observed Jesus ascending into heaven, that Jesus would return in just the same way as they saw Him leave. Jesus is coming again, and there a few more details in Revelation 19:11-21. Generally speaking, this is when those who have been true to Jesus will receive their rewards for their deeds. Believe it! He is coming again! (See 1 Corinthians 4:5, 11:26, 15:23-24; 1 Thessalonians 2:19-20, 4:15-5:4, 5:23; 2 Thessalonians 2:1-2, 8, among others which mention Jesus second coming.)

Make Disciples

Matthew 28:19-20 (NASB) "19 Go therefore and make disciples of all the nations, baptizing them in the name of the Father and the Son and the Holy Spirit, 20 teaching them to observe all that I commanded you; and lo, I am with you always, even to the end of the age." "

This statement by Jesus is usually referred to as "The Great Commission." This statement is what this book is based on—teaching the things Jesus commanded. Jesus very simply defined at least what the beginning of discipleship is all about, baptism and training in what He commanded. This book cannot baptize you, you will have to make such arrangements if not done already, but the foundation of being a disciple can result from studying these chapters and letting the Holy Spirit write His word in our hearts.

Avoid Greed and Envy

Mark 7:20-23 (NASB) "20 And He was saying, "That which proceeds out of the man, that is what defiles the man. 21 For from within, out of the heart of men, proceed the evil thoughts, fornications, thefts, murders, adulteries, 22 deeds of coveting and wickedness, as well as deceit, sensuality, envy, slander, pride and foolishness. 23 All these evil things proceed from within and defile the man." "

This is Mark's record of what was already discussed in the chapter "Evil Thoughts." It does not do any harm to reiterate the difference we must have in our heart as a Christian as opposed to what our heart was like while we were in the world. They truly are totally different kingdoms.

false Teaching and Tradition

Mark 8:15 (NASB) "15 And He was giving orders to them, saying, "Watch out! Beware of the leaven of the Pharisees and the leaven of Herod." "

Leaven is symbolic of false teaching, and the Pharisees were well known for their adherence to traditions above and beyond God's law. The religious hierarchy had added to the laws of God to a total of over 600 rules and regulations they were required to live by. God had given the Ten Commandments, some rules on sacrifices and feast and holy days, diet, and sanitation, but the Pharisees went way beyond that.

Today, we might hear the statement, "But, we've always done it that way!" That epitomizes tradition. Rules and regulations that are made by and implemented by people can quickly become false teaching, something that people have devised without God's direction nor fully based on His word. It's that "not fully based" aspect that makes it false teaching. We cannot be saved by our own works, nor by the opinion of people. An opinion cannot even save the person who comes up with the opinion. Many opinions and traditions develop because of specific economic, social, or political circumstances which only last a short time. Long after the specific situation which spawned the tradition, the tradition becomes a law to itself, even when it is not appropriate to current circumstances.

Herod was a people pleaser, He did as much as he could to keep the Jewish religious hierarchy happy, and contributed a tremendous amount of money to make the temple in Jerusalem one of the fanciest in the world at the time. The suspicion is that he did so to earn his way to heaven. It didn't work that way then, and it still does not work that way. People at the time were required to obey the commands of Herod, but, Jesus said to not behave like those in authority. (See the chapter titled, "Obey Authority.")

The basic point is that traditions can be executed without any love for God or our fellow Christians and the lost of the world. Legalism and traditions can kill in more ways than one.

Kill, Steal, False Witness

Mark 10:19 (NASB) "19 You know the commandments, 'DO not murder, DO not commit adultery, DO not steal, DO not bear false witness, Do not defraud, Honor your father and mother.'" "

These are some of the Ten Commandments, however, being a Christian does not mean we can "get away with murder." Those commandments still identify what is sin. At the last supper, Jesus made the statement, "This is the New Covenant in my blood." (Luke 22:20) In the Greek, there are two words that are translated "new." One is "neos" which means something new that has never existed before. The other is "kainos" which means something is in a different form or function. Jesus used the "kainos" word meaning that the New Covenant was based on the Old Covenant, but with a different form and function. We no longer need to make animal sacrifices for our sins is probably the most obvious difference, but, the requirement of death for sin is still in effect. It is now the shed blood of Christ that makes atonement for our sin when we believe on Jesus for salvation.

Jeremiah 31:33, Romans 2:15, Hebrews 10:16 tell us that God will write His Law on our hearts and minds as part of this New Covenant. Loving the Lord and our neighbor is part of that, but it is not restricted to that. Neither the Old Testament nor the New Testament say anything about a "Law of Love." Love fulfills the Law, but that does not make Love a Law. God's definition of sin (the Ten Commandments) is still valid for the Christian way of life, the difference being that in the Old Covenant times the Law had to be fulfilled in the strength of the flesh. In the New Covenant, the Law is fulfilled by the power of the Holy Spirit living in us. Faith was still a part of it then, as was the case with Abraham whose faith in God was credited as righteousness, but back then, the evidence of that faith was done by the strength of the flesh. (Genesis 15:6; Romans 4:3, 5, 6, 9, 11. "Believe" is a verb derived from "faith" which is a noun, both have the same root word in the Greek, "persuade.")

Nowhere in the New Testament is there any statement, nor hints that the Ten Commandments need no longer be obeyed. This is not to advocate legalism in any form, because we are to follow the new way of the Spirit, not the old way of the Law. (Romans 7:6)

Pride

Mark 10:35-45 (NASB) "35 James and John, the two sons of Zebedee, *came up to Jesus, saying, "Teacher, we want You to do for us whatever we ask of You." 36 And He said to them, "What do you want Me to do for you?" 37 They said to Him, "Grant that we may sit, one on Your right and one on Your left, in Your glory." 38 But Jesus said to them, "You do not know what you are asking. Are you able to drink the cup that I drink, or to be baptized with the baptism with which I am baptized?" 39 They said to Him, "We are able." And Jesus said to them, "The cup that I drink you shall drink; and you shall be baptized with the baptism with which I am baptized. 40 But to sit on My right or on My left, this is not Mine to give; but it is for those for whom it has been prepared." 41 Hearing this, the ten began to feel indignant with James and John. 42 Calling them to Himself, Jesus *said to them, "You know that those who are recognized as rulers of the Gentiles lord it over them; and their great men exercise authority over them. 43 But it is not this way among you, but whoever wishes to become great among you shall be your servant; 44 and whoever wishes to be first among you shall be slave of all. 45 For even the Son of Man did not come to be served, but to serve, and to give His life a ransom for many." "

James and John really exposed what was going on in their hearts — pride. The ways of the world mandate that someone must be "in charge" of whatever is happening. God's kingdom is just the opposite — everyone must be a servant of everyone else. God is the only one who can be "in charge" of whatever is going on. We are to be doing what He wants in our lives, He paid the price for our sins, and that price is something we can never pay back. We owe Him big-time! We cannot ever "order Him around."

Even in the process of evaluating the persuasion of the Holy Spirit toward believing in Jesus for eternal life, there is a humility and attitude of service of the Holy Spirit toward us—He never oppresses us (to exercise power over another), forces or pressures us, into believing on Jesus. Acts 10:38 tells us that oppression is from the Devil, not from God. There is a big difference between "lording it over" someone, and being their servant. That's the difference between the world and the kingdom of heaven, between being master and servant. Jesus even stated that His purpose was to serve and give His life as a ransom — we can do no more than to mimic our Lord and Savior. (Matthew 20:28, Mark 10:45)

Luke 14:8-11 describes Jesus directions when invited to a feast or celebration. Take a seat of low honor, and if the host moves you to a seat of higher honor, you will be publicly honored, but if you take a seat of high honor, you might be humiliated by needing to move to a seat of lower honor. Exaggerated self-importance (pride) will always result in your "balloon" being popped.

Galatians 6:1 tells us that the spiritual one confronting a sinning brother needs to be gentle and wary of falling into sin themselves. We are always being tempted to stray from God's path which can only result in sin. We are in this together and we need to support each other in humility.

Worship God Only

Luke 4:5-8 (NASB) "5 And he led Him up and showed Him all the kingdoms of the world in a moment of time. 6 And the devil said to Him, "I will give You all this domain and its glory; for it has been handed over to me, and I give it to whomever I wish. 7 Therefore if You worship before me, it shall all be Yours." 8 Jesus answered him, "It is written, 'You shall worship the Lord your God and serve Him only.'" "

After Jesus was baptized in the Jordan River by John the Baptist, the Holy Spirit led him into the wilderness where he fasted 40 days. Then Satan came and tempted him. This is the second temptation. Jesus responded to Satan simply with the Lord God is the only one to be worshiped.

This points back to part of what the first sin in mankind was — Adam and Eve in the Garden of Eden, in Genesis 3. Revelation 12:9 identifies there are four names for the same personage, dragon, devil, Satan, and serpent. The serpent who tempted Eve was none other than Satan himself. He cast doubt on what God had said, and then countered what God had said with the exact opposite. God had said that if they eat of the tree of the knowledge of good and evil, they would die. The serpent stated that they would not die. (Genesis 3:4) The serpent went on to explain what he wanted Eve to believe, that eating that fruit would make them like God, knowing good and evil. The "good and evil" part was rhetorical in a sense, and the "make them like God" could just as well been translated as "you can be your own god." That was the real temptation. The real issue was who is going to be god/God of their lives — the Lord God, or themselves. That battle has been going on with people since Adam and Eve.

Who is going to be on the "throne" of your life? You or God. As you walk with the Lord and grow in spiritual maturity you will come to realize that this battle is very real in your life. All it takes to dethrone God in your life is a simple thought such as, "I've been through this before, I know what to do." That thought simply means that you are taking over control of the situation in the strength of the flesh instead of listening to the still small voice of the Lord and letting Him guide you through the situation. You might be surprised to find out there are small but significant difference that you were not aware of but the Holy Spirit already knows things like that and can guide you through them.

We are not the "know-it-alls" that can do it all in the strength of the flesh. We need to stay humble before God and let Him lead always. This also points back to the first of the Ten Commandments, Exodus 20:3, you shall have no other gods before me. God does not change—He wants to be first in your life, and as you mature in Christ, you will understand more and more just how important that really is.

Do Not Test God

Luke 4:9-12 (NASB) "9 And he led Him to Jerusalem and had Him stand on the pinnacle of the temple, and said to Him, "If You are the Son of God, throw Yourself down from here; 10 for it is written, 'HE will command His angels concerning You to guard You,' 11 and, 'ON their hands they will bear You up, SO that You will not strike Your foot against A stone.'" 12 And Jesus answered and said to him, "It is said, 'You shall not put the Lord your God to the test.'" "

This is the third temptation of Jesus by Satan after Jesus had fasted 40 days. The word in the Greek translated "test" is a compound word. One of those words means "to make proof of." In earlier chapters, I've mentioned that we cannot "order God around." We do not have authority over God, it's the other way around. Putting God to the test is simply doing something which, in our minds, would force God to reveal Himself in such a way that it He would be proving He exists. We can't force God to reveal Himself. Attempting to do so is an arrogant assumption that we are greater than God, which we are not.

Part of this problem is that if God did such a thing, we would not have to live by faith, we would be able to live by sight. (1 Corinthians 5:7) Whatever is not from faith is sin. (Romans 14:23) This could also apply to the situation where someone is in trouble and swears to God that if they are delivered, they will do such-and-such in an attempt to repay God for His kindness. This is illustrated in Judges 11, specifically verses 29-40. Take the time to read this. Jephthah attempted to "bargain" with God to give him victory in battle and he would sacrifice the first thing that came out of his house when he returned. God does not participate in "bargaining" for anything for any reason. There is no real difference between "testing" or "tempting" God and "bargaining."

God has provided sufficient means for everyone to know He is for real, and He provided that evidence His way, not ours (Romans 1:20). The parable of Lazarus and the Rich Man ends with Abraham stating that they (Rich Man's brothers) have Moses and the prophets—if they can't believe based on that, neither would they believe if someone was raised from death. (Luke 16:19-31)

The point is that we must believe, have faith in God, and that is the basic requirement.

Love Enemies

Luke 6:27-35 (NASB) "27 "But I say to you who hear, love your enemies, do good to those who hate you, 28 bless those who curse you, pray for those who mistreat you. 29 Whoever hits you on the cheek, offer him the other also; and whoever takes away your coat, do not withhold your shirt from him either. 30 Give to everyone who asks of you, and whoever takes away what is yours, do not demand it back. 31 Treat others the same way you want them to treat you. 32 If you love those who love you, what credit is that to you? For even sinners love those who love them. 33 If you do good to those who do good to you, what credit is that to you? For even sinners do the same. 34 If you lend to those from whom you expect to receive, what credit is that to you? Even sinners lend to sinners in order to receive back the same amount. 35 But love your enemies, and do good, and lend, expecting nothing in return; and your reward will be great, and you will be sons of the Most High; for He Himself is kind to ungrateful and evil men."

This goes so drastically against the ways of the world, it isn't funny. But this is what Jesus calls us to do. Proverbs 25:21-22 and Romans 12:19-21 tells us that doing good to those who do evil against you is like heaping burning coals on their heads. We are not to take vengeance on those who do evil against us, God will take care of them in His timing, He is the judge, not us. We are to be different from the world, and in this passage, Jesus makes the point that we are to go "above and beyond" what people of the world do. If we only do the same things as the worldly people do, how would anyone determine there is something different about us because of Jesus? God wants us to be conformed to the image of His Son (Romans 8:29). Matthew 5:45 tells us that God causes rain and sun on both good and evil—we can do no less than imitate Him.

Proverbs 24:17-19 tells us to not rejoice over an evil person who stumbles because God sees what is in our heart and mind and will withhold His wrath from that evil one. That basically means that our sin can interfere with God's punishment of the wicked. In "Appendix D: Forgive," one of the points brought out is that the judgment of sin falls where the sin resides. If you are harboring that sin, guess where that judgment will fall?

Deny Yourself

Luke 9:23-25 (NASB) "23 And He was saying to them all, "If anyone wishes to come after Me, he must deny himself, and take up his cross daily and follow Me. 24 For whoever wishes to save his life will lose it, but whoever loses his life for My sake, he is the one who will save it. 25 For what is a man profited if he gains the whole world, and loses or forfeits himself?"

Deny self, take up our own cross, and do that daily. This is maybe the most extreme difference between the ways of the world and the life Christ wants us to lead. The world says we must make our own way, be our own boss (god), as the only way to become great. The way of Christ is to stay humble and dependent on God, each and every day. Jesus was able to do the things He did because He denied himself daily, and took on the burden of being humble and obedient to His Father (God). The Gospel of John records at least six times that Jesus said to His disciples that He did not say or do anything on His own initiative, but only did what God the Father told Him to say or do. (John 5:30; 8:28, 42; 10:18; 12:49: 14:10) We need to be the same way in everything we do and say. I'm not saying that is an easy thing to do. We battle the temptation to be our own god in every situation we encounter. But trust me, my own experience tells me that it does get easier as time goes on.

Prayer

Luke 11:1-4 (NASB) "1 It happened that while Jesus was praying in a certain place, after He had finished, one of His disciples said to Him, "Lord, teach us to pray just as John also taught his disciples." 2 And He said to them, "When you pray, say: 'Father, hallowed be Your name. Your kingdom come. 3 'Give us each day our daily bread. 4 'And forgive us our sins, For we ourselves also forgive everyone who is indebted to us. And lead us not into temptation.'" "

Matthew 6:7-13 (NASB) "7 "And when you are praying, do not use meaningless repetition as the Gentiles do, for they suppose that they will be heard for their many words. 8 So do not be like them; for your Father knows what you need before you ask Him. 9 "Pray, then, in this way: 'Our Father who is in heaven, Hallowed be Your name. 10 'Your kingdom come. Your will be done, On earth as it is in heaven. 11 'Give us this day our daily bread. 12 'And forgive us our debts, as we also have forgiven our debtors. 13 'And do not lead us into temptation, but deliver us from evil. [For Yours is the kingdom and the power and the glory forever. Amen.']"

This is commonly known as "The Lord's Prayer." (In the NASB, words in brackets, "[]" are words found in some manuscripts, but not necessarily the oldest.) Some congregations recite this as a normal part of their Sunday worship service, there is nothing wrong with that. Jesus gave this prayer as a model for His disciples.

This prayer can be "broken down" into its parts, such as: addressing God as our Father, declaring His holiness, humility in declaring His will is more important than our own, request to provide our needs on a daily basis, request for forgiveness of our sins as we forgive other's sins against us, request for deliverance from the end results that evil wants to impose on us.

The first parts are usually called praise and worship of God for who He is. Then an admission of humility and submission to God's will because He provided the payment for our sins which we are incapable of paying ourselves or paying Him back. Then whatever needs we may have, and this can and should include anything in our lives at the moment. Forgiveness for our sins is next, and note carefully that forgiveness of our own sins is dependent on our forgiveness of the sins of others done against ourselves. The last part is a request to be rescued from the end result of any evil schemes of the Devil (See Ephesians chapter 6, the full armor of God). Those things are going to come our way, but God can deliver us from the intended results.

In respect to forgiveness, look up the following verses and think about them a while: Matthew 11:25-26, 18:21-35; 1 John 1:9; Colossians 3:13; James 5:14-16. See "Appendix D: Forgive," for an in-depth analysis of what the word "forgive" means and how it is implemented in our lives.

Don't Hide Your Light

Luke 11:33-36 (NASB) "33 "No one, after lighting a lamp, puts it away in a cellar nor under a basket, but on the lampstand, so that those who enter may see the light. 34 The eye is the lamp of your body; when your eye is clear, your whole body also is full of light; but when it is bad, your body also is full of darkness. 35 Then watch out that the light in you is not darkness. 36 If therefore your whole body is full of light, with no dark part in it, it will be wholly illumined, as when the lamp illumines you with its rays." "

Darkness in our lives can come from many sources such as bad teaching that does not line up with what is actually written in the original languages of Scripture, dependence on rules and regulations instead of faith, letting your heart be over burdened by the cares of the world, habits from our life before we found salvation in Jesus, etc. The point Jesus is making here is that we need to avoid those things that interfere with God's work in our lives. We need to confront them and overcome them as indicated in 1 John 4:1-4.

In Acts 17:10-12 it is described for us that the Bereans listened to Paul, then went and researched the Scriptures to verify that what Paul had said was true. Verifying that what is preached or taught is true and accurate to Scripture is something that everyone should be doing. This is the critical point, people can be wrong, God is not wrong, but people can mess things up—even our congregational leaders.

It is important for us to pray for our leaders in our congregations so that they can accurately teach us from God's word. It can be very easy for us to read anything, including God's word with filters in our minds and hearts based on traditions without really recognizing we are doing so. There is nothing wrong with questioning God about something we read in the bible that we have problems understanding. God will honor sincere questions about His word so that we can grow closer to Him and be a beacon to others about God's love and the salvation we have found in Jesus.

Do Justice and Love God

Luke 11:42 (NASB) "42 "But woe to you Pharisees! For you pay tithe of mint and rue and every kind of garden herb, and yet disregard justice and the love of God; but these are the things you should have done without neglecting the others."

The Pharisees, it turns out, were good examples of bad religion. Way back in Genesis, Cain and Able made sacrifices to God. Cain's sacrifice was not acceptable to God, and in the least, Cain was not happy about it. Cain offered the fruit of plants, Able offered a blood sacrifice in line with the blood sacrifice God made for Adam and Eve. (Genesis 3:21) Here in Luke 11,the Pharisees are following the bad example of Cain instead of seeking God's justice and love, and doing things His way. Seeking God's justice and love, and giving that to others is more important than offering questionable sacrifices.

Everything will be exposed

Luke 12:1-5 (NASB) "1 Under these circumstances, after so many thousands of people had gathered together that they were stepping on one another, He began saying to His disciples first of all, "Beware of the leaven of the Pharisees, which is hypocrisy. 2 But there is nothing covered up that will not be revealed, and hidden that will not be known. 3 Accordingly, whatever you have said in the dark will be heard in the light, and what you have whispered in the inner rooms will be proclaimed upon the housetops. 4 "I say to you, My friends, do not be afraid of those who kill the body and after that have no more that they can do. 5 But I will warn you whom to fear: fear the One who, after He has killed, has authority to cast into hell; yes, I tell you, fear Him!"

Hypocrisy is simply acting as something you are not. When you see someone at church on Sunday being all nice and smiley, and then at work during the week that person is an irritable, difficult person—that is hypocrisy. God already knows that kind of thing is going on, and it will be revealed. Nothing is hidden from God, and He is the one who has authority to cast into hell. Don't be a phony, if there is something you recognize as wrong in your life, deal with it even if you have to get other Christians to help you with it. Matthew 15:18 and Luke 6:45 tell us that what comes out of our mouth comes from our heart. What we say and how we behave reveals our true nature. The Pharisees did and said things that were contradictory to each other, revealing their true nature. In Matthew 23:27, Jesus calls them "whitewashed tombs," pretty on the outside and full of uncleanness on the inside. We need to listen to ourselves and make certain that what we speak reveals God's righteousness in our hearts.

Denying Jesus

Luke 12:8-12 (NASB) "8 "And I say to you, everyone who confesses Me before men, the Son of Man will confess him also before the angels of God; 9 but he who denies Me before men will be denied before the angels of God. 10 And everyone who speaks a word against the Son of Man, it will be forgiven him; but he who blasphemes against the Holy Spirit, it will not be forgiven him. 11 When they bring you before the synagogues and the rulers and the authorities, do not worry about how or what you are to speak in your defense, or what you are to say; 12 for the Holy Spirit will teach you in that very hour what you ought to say." "

This discussion of Jesus may seem to wander a bit. There are three areas covered: denying Jesus, blasphemy, and how to handle persecution. The first is fairly simple and straight forward. If the Holy Spirit has given us eternal life, we will confess Jesus before others, if one does not have eternal life, that person will not confess Jesus before others. (1 Corinthians 12:3) This is the basis for the third part of what Jesus is saying, but let's cover things in the order provided.

Blasphemy is ascribing something of Satan or evil to God. Matthew 12:24-28 describes Jesus being accused by the religious leaders of casting out demons by the power of Beelzebul (Satan). Jesus uses this accusation to discuss blasphemy. Jesus was doing something holy and righteous, but the leaders ascribed it to Satan. Blasphemy against Jesus and God the Father can be forgiven (note "can"), but ascribing the work of the Holy Spirit to Satan or evil will not be forgiven. Mark 3:28-30 defines it as an eternal sin. (See also Luke 12:10)

Jesus then switches to a description of persecution—being brought before the authorities because of the name of Christ. If we are to endure persecution, even if it results in our death, we must confess Jesus Christ, which can only be done by the Holy Spirit dwelling in us. For that to happen, we can never ascribe anything even remotely evil to the work of the Holy Spirit. The history of the early Church is recorded in the book of Acts. There are several instances where the Apostles and disciples were brought before the religious authorities because they were preaching Jesus. They had to rely on the still small voice of the Lord all through the inquisitions. If they had depended on the strength of the flesh, the ingenuity of their own minds, it would have turned out miserably different than what actually happened.

The same goes for us today. We may experience a different level of persecution than what took place in the book of Acts, however, no matter the level of intensity, we must confess Jesus. There are no alternatives.

Jesus First

Luke 14:26-33 (NASB) "26 "If anyone comes to Me, and does not hate his own father and mother and wife and children and brothers and sisters, yes, and even his own life, he cannot be My disciple. 27 Whoever does not carry his own cross and come after Me cannot be My disciple. 28 For which one of you, when he wants to build a tower, does not first sit down and calculate the cost to see if he has enough to complete it? 29 Otherwise, when he has laid a foundation and is not able to finish, all who observe it begin to ridicule him, 30 saying, 'This man began to build and was not able to finish.' 31 Or what king, when he sets out to meet another king in battle, will not first sit down and consider whether he is strong enough with ten thousand men to encounter the one coming against him with twenty thousand? 32 Or else, while the other is still far away, he sends a delegation and asks for terms of peace. 33 So then, none of you can be My disciple who does not give up all his own possessions."

Hate seems like a strong term here, however, it is a relative term. Jesus must be more important than any of our relatives or even ourselves. Not that we ignore our family and mistreat them, we are to care for our family just as the early church cared for any who had need. Several times, the Apostle Paul describes how a man raises his children and the overall behavior of his family as qualifications for being a leader in the local congregation. (1 Timothy 3:1-13, Titus 1:5-9)

We have probably heard the term "count the cost," and this is the crux of the matter. Are you willing to have your family hate you for being a Christian? Sometimes this happens if a child in the family finds salvation in Jesus, and the rest of the family shuns them. There is a burden to bear for being a Christian. Matthew

11:30 tells us that His yoke is easy and His burden is light. Even a light burden is a burden. Matthew chapter 13 has recorded many statements of Jesus about what the kingdom of heaven is like. Take the time to read His descriptions — many of them go along with the illustration of building a tower or fighting a war and its associated costs. The kingdom of heaven is definitely worth the cost in the overall perspective. Don't let the cares of the world choke things out as Jesus identified in the parable of the seeds and soils in Matthew 13:1-23. (See chapter, "Persecution, Cares of the World."

In many situations in life we need to make a careful assessment of what is most important and are we willing to pay the cost.

When a Brother Sins

Luke 17:3-4 (NASB) "3 Be on your guard! If your brother sins, rebuke him; and if he repents, forgive him. 4 And if he sins against you seven times a day, and returns to you seven times, saying, 'I repent,' forgive him." "

In our current English dialect, the word "rebuke" seems kind of harsh. To a point, it could be harsh. It means "to assess strictly," meaning that something is or is not, and there are no degrees of possibility between is or is not. It does not require anger or vicious language for communicating. We superimpose a bad (harsh) attitude on it. There are several times in the Gospels where Jesus had stated something and the disciples questioned it, seemingly not understanding when they should have understood after so many years of being with Jesus. Jesus replied to the effect of, "You still don't understand yet?" I seriously doubt that He shouted that in anger, bewilderment maybe, but not anger. The whole point of forgiving that brother must be based on love. The world is supposed to know Jesus lives in us by our love for each other, not our anger. (John 13:35) When we talk to someone else about their sin, we must do so in gentleness, watching out for ourselves to not become entrapped in the same kind of snare. (Matthew 18:15-17; Galatians 6:1; 2 Thessalonians 3:15; James 5:19-20)

The point is to confront sin in another on the basis of love, just like God did with us by sending Jesus to die on the cross for our sins. People may shout the "gospel" with fire and brimstone, but that is not the way Jesus did it, and the persuasion of the Holy Spirit is gentle but direct. We need to be the same, even when that brother needs to be forgiven many times a day. (See also chapter titled "Forgive How Much?")

Believe the Prophets

Luke 24:25 (NASB) "25 And He said to them, "O foolish men and slow of heart to believe in all that the prophets have spoken!"

This is a response by Jesus about the doubt and bewilderment expressed by those who went to the tomb after He had risen from death. Jesus himself had prophesied about his death and resurrection in very clear terms directly to His disciples, and they still did not understand it. The death of Christ was prophesied in the Old Testament, Isaiah 53 is probably the most descriptive of what the Messiah would go through in order to die for sins. Psalm 16:10 indicates that God will not let His holy one see corruption—in that time frame seeing corruption only meant the decay of a dead corpse. So, God not letting corruption take place could only mean resurrection from death. There are no verses in the Old Testament which specifically state in so many blunt words that Messiah would be raised from death.1 Corinthians 2:8 tells us why—the evil rulers of the heavenlies would not have crucified Christ if they had known God's plan of resurrection. In spite of that, God did give us one small clue…

Be Born Again

John 3:3 (NASB) "3 Jesus answered and said to him, "Truly, truly, I say to you, unless one is born again he cannot see the kingdom of God." "

God's kingdom is the context of existence for eternal life. When we are born physically, we are born sinners, separated from God. David in Psalm 51 identified he was conceived in sin. We are not born sinless, but full blown sinners, wanting to be god of our own lives. (See "Appendix B: The New Birth") This is the only way to eternal life, God's kingdom, the kingdom of heaven.

John 3:15-16 (NASB) "15 so that whoever believes will in Him have eternal life. 16 "For God so loved the world, that He gave His only begotten Son, that whoever believes in Him shall not perish, but have eternal life."

Believing in Jesus is the only way to be born again. This is also identified in Matthew 18:3 among many other verses. You are reading this book because you have already believed in Jesus for eternal life.

Think of it this way: what would be the point of becoming part of God's kingdom and still having to deal with the problem of sin? This is the point that was missed by the Jewish leaders (and people) back in bible times, both Old and New Testament times. God takes care of things in their proper order. Believing in Jesus is the starting point so we can live eternally in His kingdom without the burden of having to continually deal with sin..

Jesus · Messiah

John 4:23-26 (NASB) "23 But an hour is coming, and now is, when the true worshipers will worship the Father in spirit and truth; for such people the Father seeks to be His worshipers. 24 God is spirit, and those who worship Him must worship in spirit and truth. 25 The woman *said to Him, "I know that Messiah is coming (He who is called Christ); when that One comes, He will declare all things to us." 26 Jesus *said to her, "I who speak to you am He." "

"Messiah" in the Hebrew means "anointed one." The Greek "Christ" means the same thing. The word Messiah is only used four times in the Old Testament, Psalm 2:2, 72:2; Daniel 9:25, 26. Based on Daniel's writings, the first century Jew was looking forward to the coming Messiah. Here in John, we have Jesus declaring that He is that expected one.

To this day, the Jews don't put much, if any, weight to Isaiah 53 which describes the suffering of God's anointed one that was completely fulfilled by Jesus. In addition to Isaiah 53, the miracles done by Jesus should have been more than enough to "prove" who Jesus really is. It seems the Jewish mindset of the first century leaned more toward a conquering warrior general than a suffering servant and they completely missed it. This mindset is most likely the reason the disciples in Acts 1 asked Jesus if now was when the kingdom would be restored to Israel—to which Jesus relied that it was not for them to know God's timing.

Think of it in these terms. Salvation makes us members in the kingdom of heaven. Salvation also removes sin and its effects from us so we can follow God for eternity without any encumbrance from sin and its effects. Could you imagine the confusion and continued problems we would each encounter if sin was not taken care of first, before we enter the kingdom in eternity?

True worship of God/Messiah will only happen when done in Spirit and truth. By "Spirit" what is meant is actually praying or worshiping in the Spirit. Ephesians 6:18 tells us we are to pray in the Spirit. (At the most basic level that means not doing it in the strength of the flesh.) That worship also takes place on the basis of the truth of His word, not the traditions of people or opinions of the fleshly mind.

Historical Note: The following is based on historical writings, not what is contained in the bible—please keep that in mind. The High Priest and the Temple priests and Rabbis, around the time Jesus was 6-9 years old, established a committee to go throughout Israel and search for anyone who had been born around the right time according to their records. Their purpose was to determine if the Messiah had actually arrived. This committee actually interviewed Mary, Joseph, and Jesus, and dismissed Jesus as a potential for being the Messiah. They got that close and still missed it. (From "The Archko Volume or the Archaeological Writings of the Sanhedrin and Talmuds of the Jews", chapter V, "Gamaliel's interview with Joseph and Mary and others concerning Jesus", originally published around 1880. Although there may be some inconsistencies in some of the information regarding Constantine in this book, the book does reveal a lot about the first century Jewish mindset.)

Do Not Sin Anymore

John 5:2-8 (NASB) "2 Now there is in Jerusalem by the sheep gate a pool, which is called in Hebrew Bethesda, having five porticoes. 3 In these lay a multitude of those who were sick, blind, lame, and withered, [waiting for the moving of the waters; 4 for an angel of the Lord went down at certain seasons into the pool and stirred up the water; whoever then first, after the stirring up of the water, stepped in was made well from whatever disease with which he was afflicted.] 5 A man was there who had been ill for thirty-eight years. 6 When Jesus saw him lying there, and knew that he had already been a long time in that condition, He *said to him, "Do you wish to get well?" 7 The sick man answered Him, "Sir, I have no man to put me into the pool when the water is stirred up, but while I am coming, another steps down before me." 8 Jesus *said to him, "Get up, pick up your pallet and walk."

John 5:14 (NASB) 14 Afterward Jesus *found him in the temple and said to him, "Behold, you have become well; do not sin anymore, so that nothing worse happens to you." "

Jesus admonition to the man healed at the Pool of Bethesda is simply "do not sin anymore." This is not the only time this admonition was made. (John 8:11) This is a difficult command to follow, simple, but difficult. 1 John 2:1 also tells us that we are to not sin, but if we do, we can find forgiveness in Jesus.

In the NASB the word "lawlessness" is used 14 times, twice in the Old Testament, 12 in the New. Two of the verses in the NT simply say that lawlessness is sin, and sin is lawlessness—neither of these really explain what is lawlessness. Some of the other 10 verses talk about the Internet of the heart as part of lawlessness. The best definition of lawlessness I've found is: "the intent of the heart to commit sin." This makes lawlessness the opposite of righteousness, "the intent of the heart to pursue holiness." This is really where sin (separation from God) resides, in our hearts. As has been discussed in other chapters, it is what comes out of our hearts that defiles us.

To not sin must become part of our heart. This must be a prominent desire of our heart.

Study God's Word

John 5:39-40 (NASB) "39 You search the Scriptures because you think that in them you have eternal life; it is these that testify about Me; 40 and you are unwilling to come to Me so that you may have life."

This may seem a bit strange, considering the way we talk about things in our modern American English. The words written in what we call the bible are just simply words. I have read things by atheists regarding the bible. They have read the words in the bible, but there is no salvation in the atheist. Salvation is found in Jesus. The words written in the bible are the most important words ever written in the world, but words on paper are simply words on paper. It is when, because of those words, we seek Jesus, that the Holy Spirit takes those words and uses them to persuade us to believe in Jesus. Once we find salvation in Jesus, the Holy Spirit writes the words of the bible on our hearts, part of the conversion process that takes a lifetime (Matthew 18:3). The difference between an atheist and a Christian is that the Christian has permitted the Holy Spirit to persuade them to believe in Jesus using the words written in the bible and let the Holy Spirit come into their spirit providing eternal life, the atheist does not.

In Romans 2:8, the word "obey" is used twice. Both times it is a derivative of the word "persuade" in the Greek. Using the word persuade in this verse it reads, 'but to those who are selfishly ambitious and refuse to be persuaded to the truth, but are persuaded to unrighteousness, wrath and indignation.' The Scriptures are words that the Holy Spirit uses to persuade us to believe in Jesus for salvation, and then uses them to persuade us to continue to follow in Jesus' footsteps.

That continuance depends on our studying the Scriptures. David made the statement, "Your word I have hidden in my heart so that I will not sin against You." (Psalm 119:11) Studying the bible keeps you on track to mature into the Christian God wants you to be.

Judge Righteously

John 7:24 (NASB) "24 "Do not judge according to appearance, but judge with righteous judgment." "

The modern US English version of this is, "Don't judge a book by its cover." Righteous judgment can only be accomplished by God Himself, and then by us when we listen to the "still small voice of the Lord." (1 Kings 19:11-13) The world wants to condemn on superficial whims and punish (aside from blatant violations of the law). The ways of God require us to follow His righteousness. 1 Samuel 16:7 tells us that God looks on the heart, people can only see the outside of a person. People are going to screw up—guaranteed. We can have the best intentions in the universe, and it just won't go right. Others will look at our failure and totally ignore any initial purpose for why we started what we did. That is what Jesus is saying here—God can see the intent of our heart, and that is what we will be judged on, partly. In God's scheme of things, the end does not justify the means—the means must be just as holy and righteous as the end goal. We need to do things God's way, not our way in the strength of the flesh. When God, through the Holy Spirit dwelling within us, provides the strength, boldness, guidance, direction, etc., then, and only then, can the outward appearance look righteous. There may still be some who judge harshly, but at this point it can only be because they just don't like godly activities and results. God is the righteous, reliable judge, and His judgment is the only thing that really matters. We must follow His judgment, not out own.

Jesus is the I AM of Exodus

John 8:24 (NASB) "24 "Therefore I said to you that you will die in your sins; for unless you believe that I am He, you will die in your sins." "

The "He" in the quote from Exodus 3:14 is added by the translators and is not in the original Greek text. This is a typical first century manner of speaking, or a figure of speech. God revealed Himself to Moses as simply "I AM." That means in simple terms that God has always existed and will always exist, was never created—is self-existent. This means that Jesus is God in the flesh. God is the only one who could provide a blameless sacrifice for all our sins, the sins of the whole world (1 John 2:2). The Old Testament Law had to be fulfilled in the strength of the flesh, and everyone fails that (except Jesus). Jesus is fully God and fully man, all at the same time. The difference between Jesus and everybody else is that Jesus fully obeyed God the Father. It was mentioned in an earlier chapter that in the Gospel of John, Jesus stated, at least a half dozen times, that He does nothing of His own initiative, but only does what the Father tells Him to do or say. We need to believe that Jesus is God the son. The gospel of John begins by describing Jesus as the Word of God from the beginning of everything. Jesus spoke the universe into existence, and everything that follows. When we believe in Jesus, we believe in God.

Continued Obedience

John 8:31-32 (NASB) "31 So Jesus was saying to those Jews who had believed Him, "If you continue in My word, then you are truly disciples of Mine; 32 and you will know the truth, and the truth will make you free." "

Continuing to believe, and be obedient to what Jesus has provided in the bible by the inspiration of the Holy Spirit is an indicator that we are truly disciples. This continuation in His word is what allows us to know the truth and be truly free.

In both English and first century Greek, this is a conditional statement, "If you continue..." Jesus never describes anything that would qualify as a label for the person who does not continue. Not continuing should not be an option for us. Could it happen that someone starts and does not finish? Yes, In the parable discussed in an earlier chapter regarding seeds and soils, there was the third type that grew up but got distracted by the cares and worries of the world (choked by the thorns and thistles). The book you are reading is a good start on knowing what Jesus has said and finding the ability to continue in His word.

The freedom Jesus is talking about is being free from the burden of sin and the impending judgment/punishment that comes with it. Freedom does not mean we can now do anything we want—some of those "wants" would either be outright sin or lead to sin, which we are not to do. Freedom comes in knowing (from studying and continuing in His word) what can lead to sin and deliberately choosing to shun that, and instead, do what is righteous. We encounter situations every day which require our decision based on His righteousness.

Love One Another

John 13:34-35 (NASB) "34 "A new commandment I give to you, that you love one another, even as I have loved you, that you also love one another. 35 By this all men will know that you are My disciples, if you have love for one another." "

Following the previous chapter on continuing in His word so we can truly be His disciples, comes the admonition to love one another so others can see that we are His disciples. These two factors hit both horizontal and vertical relations.

In this verse, the word in the Greek for love (agape) means, "To have love for someone or something, based on sincere appreciation and high regard, a matter of will and action toward the object of love" In other words, this love is not based on what the object of love has done or "earned." We love Him because He first loved us, is one way of applying 1 John 4:19-21 (which repeats some of what Jesus says here). We must realize that God has loved us when we were unlovable, totally absorbed in sin. Loving God with that understanding should be the obvious response. He loved us with agape love—we respond because of His love for us.

This is also an application of what Jesus says are the greatest two commandments, love God with all your heart, mind, soul, strength, and love your neighbor as yourself. In this case, the "neighbor" includes your "brother" in the Lord. (Matthew 22:36-40; Mark 12:30-31)

Exodus 20:6 (NASB) "6 but showing lovingkindness to thousands, to those who love Me and keep My commandments."

This shows us that this concept of love has been consistent throughout time—one of the unchangeable attributes of God. Jesus wants us to continue that attribute towards God and others.

Keep His Commands

John 14:15 (NASB) "15 "If you love Me, you will keep My commandments."

Matthew 7:21-23 (NASB) "21 "Not everyone who says to Me, 'Lord, Lord,' will enter the kingdom of heaven, but he who does the will of My Father who is in heaven will enter. 22 Many will say to Me on that day, 'Lord, Lord, did we not prophesy in Your name, and in Your name cast out demons, and in Your name perform many miracles?' 23 And then I will declare to them, 'I never knew you; depart from ME, you who practice lawlessness.' "

When we love someone, we want to do things for them, we want to do what makes them happy. At the same time, there is a real selfish aspect to this—we want to hear Jesus say to us, "Well done good and faithful servant, enter into the joy of your master." (From the parable of the talents.) See "Appendix C: Completing the work Christ gives us" for more on this aspect. The point of this verse, is that keeping the things Jesus has commanded us is an expression of our love for Him.

Romans 8:29 tells us that God wants us to be conformed to the image of His Son. Following, and obeying, the commands He has given us is part of the change from the ways of the world to the ways of God that He wants us to be conformed to. (See Matthew 19:17; John 15:10; 1 Timothy 8:14; 1 John 2:3, 4, 3:22, 5:3; Revelation 12:17, 14:12)

Jesus brings this point to a startling reality in Matthew 7:21-23. Here He identifies that the future residents of heaven are those who do the will of the Father. And those who do not do the will of the Father are sent away. The best definition of "lawlessness" is: "the intent of the heart to commit sin." That makes lawlessness the opposite of righteousness, "the intent of the heart to pursue holiness." Pursuing holiness requires obedience, which is essential to keeping His commands.

It's interesting to note that several times in Revelation the members of the "churches" are identified as those who keep Christ's commandments. (See chapter, "Revelation Prophecies.")

Receive the Holy Spirit

John 20:22 (NASB) "22 And when He had said this, He breathed on them and *said to them, "Receive the Holy Spirit." "

This takes place the evening of Christ's resurrection. The statement Jesus made when He breathed on them is written in such a way that it means: "Right there, right then, they received the Holy Spirit, and the Holy Spirit continued with them." This is when they were sealed with the Holy Spirit for eternal life. The other verses that discuss being sealed with the Holy Spirit are 2 Corinthians 1:22; Ephesians 1:13, 4:30. This encounter with the Holy Spirit is different than the one which happened 50 days later in the upper room, described in Acts chapter 2.

Jesus described their second encounter with the Holy Spirit in Luke 24:48-49, and Acts 1:8, as being given power, not eternal life, "clothed with power," and "you will receive power," are the phrases Jesus used. Let's dig into this a bit. What does clothing do for people, aside from the not being naked aspect? An illustration to answer that is: pick any day in January and fly to Minneapolis MN, and walk out of the terminal wearing flip-flops, shorts, and a T-shirt, are you properly clothed to handle the environment you must deal with? The rhetorical answer is obviously "No!" Clothing helps us interface with our environment. What was the environment the disciples had to deal with? Being able to boldly preach the gospel, and endure the persecution which was going to hit them very soon. And clothing is worn on the outside, not on or in our heart and spirit.

When we find salvation in Jesus, we need to understand, usually after the fact, that eternal life is the Holy Spirit living in our spirit. That is the key to becoming a part of God's kingdom. This "new birth" was only possible after Jesus was raised from death— Jesus was the first, His disciples were next that same day. This is the first step that takes place when we believe in Jesus for salvation.

78

God Has Cleansed the Unclean

Acts 10:9-16 (NASB) "9 On the next day, as they were on their way and approaching the city, Peter went up on the housetop about the sixth hour to pray. 10 But he became hungry and was desiring to eat; but while they were making preparations, he fell into a trance; 11 and he *saw the sky opened up, and an object like a great sheet coming down, lowered by four corners to the ground, 12 and there were in it all kinds of four-footed animals and crawling creatures of the earth and birds of the air. 13 A voice came to him, "Get up, Peter, kill and eat!" 14 But Peter said, "By no means, Lord, for I have never eaten anything unholy and unclean." 15 Again a voice came to him a second time, "What God has cleansed, no longer consider unholy." 16 This happened three times, and immediately the object was taken up into the sky."

This is also documented in Acts chapter 11 when Peter reported back to the Elders in Jerusalem regarding the trip to Cornelius's house (the first major Gentile group receiving the gospel after Pentecost). Here, Peter has a vision from God which declares that what had been unclean is now declared clean. "Clean," is according to the Old Testament Law descriptions of what foods and things they were allowed to touch and eat and what they were not allowed to touch and eat.

This vision precipitated a major paradigm shift in the early church. Initially, the only people who heard the gospel message were Jews. God had promised Abraham that through his seed all the peoples would be blessed, not just Abraham's immediate bloodline (Genesis 12:1-3). Unfortunately, the Jews were very selfish and protective of what they were supposed to have and guard. Gentiles were treated as social lepers, and any Jewish boy or girl that married a Gentile was considered dead and the family held a funeral service for them. Now, God was reaching out to the Gentiles with the gospel and that required breaking the old paradigm and instituting a new one.

The gospel is for everyone no matter what their ethnic origin or where they live on Earth. No one is "unclean" anymore. Everyone is welcome to believe on Jesus for salvation.

Communion

Luke 22:17-20 (NASB) "17 And when He had taken a cup and given thanks, He said, "Take this and share it among yourselves; 18 for I say to you, I will not drink of the fruit of the vine from now on until the kingdom of God comes." 19 And when He had taken some bread and given thanks, He broke it and gave it to them, saying, "This is My body which is given for you; do this in remembrance of Me." 20 And in the same way He took the cup after they had eaten, saying, "This cup which is poured out for you is the new covenant in My blood."

1 Corinthians 11:23-31 (NASB) "23 For I received from the Lord that which I also delivered to you, that the Lord Jesus in the night in which He was betrayed took bread; 24 and when He had given thanks, He broke it and said, "This is My body, which is for you; do this in remembrance of Me." 25 In the same way He took the cup also after supper, saying, "This cup is the new covenant in My blood; do this, as often as you drink it, in remembrance of Me." 26 For as often as you eat this bread and drink the cup, you proclaim the Lord's death until He comes.

27 Therefore whoever eats the bread or drinks the cup of the Lord in an unworthy manner, shall be guilty of the body and the blood of the Lord. 28 But a man must examine himself, and in so doing he is to eat of the bread and drink of the cup. 29 For he who eats and drinks, eats and drinks judgment to himself if he does not judge the body rightly. 30 For this reason many among you are weak and sick, and a number sleep. 31 But if we judged ourselves rightly, we would not be judged."

What is called "The Lord's Supper" is also recorded in Matthew 26:26-29 and Mark 14:22-25. The passage in 1 Corinthians was given to Paul by God, and it matches the gospel accounts. We are simply directed to "do this in remembrance" of Jesus. The modern, common, name for this is Communion. Various congregations practice this on various schedules/ The schedule is not what is important, the doing is what is important.

Shortly before Jesus was crucified, he made a statement in the area of the Temple in Jerusalem that people needed to eat His flesh and drink His blood to enter the kingdom of heaven. (John 6:52-29) Jesus was not talking about cannibalism. He was symbolically referring to the scientific fact as we know it now, that when we eat, the nutrients from food get to each and every cell in our body. Finding salvation in Jesus is to affect and permeate every part of us and every aspect of our lives. No part of us is to be left out, all of us is included.

When we take communion, it is supposed to be a reminder of what Jesus sacrificed so that we can have forgiveness of our sins, and eternal life with God. Never forget this or take it for granted.

Be on the Alert

Matthew 24:42-44 (NASB) "42 "Therefore be on the alert, for you do not know which day your Lord is coming. 43 But be sure of this, that if the head of the house had known at what time of the night the thief was coming, he would have been on the alert and would not have allowed his house to be broken into. 44 For this reason you also must be ready; for the Son of Man is coming at an hour when you do not think He will."

Matthew 25:13 (NASB) "13 Be on the alert then, for you do not know the day nor the hour."

Mark 13:33-37 (NASB) "33 "Take heed, keep on the alert; for you do not know when the appointed time will come. 34 It is like a man away on a journey, who upon leaving his house and putting his slaves in charge, assigning to each one his task, also commanded the doorkeeper to stay on the alert. 35 Therefore, be on the alert—for you do not know when the master of the house is coming, whether in the evening, at midnight, or when the rooster crows, or in the morning— 36 in case he should come suddenly and find you asleep. 37 What I say to you I say to all, 'Be on the alert!'" "

Luke 12:37 (NASB) "37 Blessed are those slaves whom the master will find on the alert when he comes; truly I say to you, that he will gird himself to serve, and have them recline at the table, and will come up and wait on them."

Luke 21:36 (NASB) "36 But keep on the alert at all times, praying that you may have strength to escape all these things that are about to take place, and to stand before the Son of Man." "

Each of these references points to the second coming of Christ. We need to keep on the alert because:

Mark 13:32 (NASB)" 32 But of that day or hour no one

knows, not even the angels in heaven, nor the Son, but the Father alone."

Only God the Father knows when that day will come. In Revelation chapter 1, there are two references to the time these things (End Times) will happen, 1:1, 3. The time phrases are: "the things which must soon take place;" and "for the time is near." The obvious time words are "soon" and "near." These are different words in the Greek. The word for soon in some versions is translated "quickly." It comes from a Greek word from which we get our English word "tachometer," how many revolutions per minute is your car engine turning? In this context (Revelation) it means that what is going to take place will not take a whole lot of time to accomplish. The other word, "near," is different in the Greek, and is a vague reference to time. It cannot be "pinned down" to a moment, hour, month, year, century, millennium, or whatever.

Here's an illustration to help us understand the difference. Picture the End Time judgments as a loaded pistol with the hammer cocked. We do not know when God the Father will pull the trigger, but we know it is "near." When He does pull that trigger, the bullet will proceed "quickly" and take care of its intended purpose.

We are always to be watchful for Christ's second coming.

Matthew 24:45-46 (NASB) "45 "Who then is the faithful and sensible slave whom his master put in charge of his household to give them their food at the proper time? 46 Blessed is that slave whom his master finds so doing when he comes."

We are to be about God's business all the time because we really do not know how much longer we have to accomplish what work He has given us (See "Appendix C: Completing the work Christ gives us").

Revelation Prophecies

Revelation 22:7 (NASB) "7 "And behold, I am coming quickly. Blessed is he who heeds the words of the prophecy of this book."

I am not aware of anyone in their right mind that would deliberately refuse a blessing for not paying attention to some words. Yes, Revelation has a LOT of words, but it is understandable. Revelation gives us the first BIG clue as to what God is going to have us doing shortly after the Rapture. God has provided the vision of Revelation so that we have a "context" for understanding how and why God is discipling us. That is something the enemy of our souls does not want us to find out so that we don't fulfill what God wants to do in our lives—preparation for eternity.

The book: "Revelation: A Fresh Perspective," organizes Revelation using only simple reading fundamentals like, "context," "definition," "logic," "history," "proper inference," "consistency," etc. It does not use academic hermeneutical mumbo-jumbo (complicated methodologies to interpret the Bible). It is not a "quick" read because there are so many details in that vision. However, it does make sense out of Revelation like no other book on the market.

Appendix A: Using what God gives us

Matthew 25:14-30 (NASB) "14 "For it is just like a man about to go on a journey, who called his own slaves and entrusted his possessions to them. 15 To one he gave five talents, to another, two, and to another, one, each according to his own ability; and he went on his journey. 16 Immediately the one who had received the five talents went and traded with them, and gained five more talents. 17 In the same manner the one who had received the two talents gained two more. 18 But he who received the one talent went away, and dug a hole in the ground and hid his master's money. 19 "Now after a long time the master of those slaves *came and *settled accounts with them. 20 The one who had received the five talents came up and brought five more talents, saying, 'Master, you entrusted five talents to me. See, I have gained five more talents.' 21 His master said to him, 'Well done, good and faithful slave. You were faithful with a few things, I will put you in charge of many things; enter into the joy of your master.' 22 "Also the one who had received the two talents came up and said, 'Master, you entrusted two talents to me. See, I have gained two more talents.' 23 His master said to him, 'Well done, good and faithful slave. You were faithful with a few things, I will put you in charge of many things; enter into the joy of your master.' 24 "And the one also who had received the one talent came up and said, 'Master, I knew you to be a hard man, reaping where you did not sow and gathering where you scattered no seed. 25 And I was afraid, and went away and hid your talent in the ground. See, you have what is yours.' 26 "But his master answered and said to him, 'You wicked, lazy slave, you knew that I reap where I did not sow and gather where I scattered no seed. 27 Then you ought to have put my money in the bank, *and on my arrival I would have received my money back with interest. 28 Therefore take away the talent from him, and give it to the one who has the ten talents.' 29 "For to everyone who has, more shall be given, and he will have an abundance; but from the one who does not have, even what he does have shall be taken away. 30 Throw out the worthless slave into the outer darkness; in that place there will be weeping and gnashing of teeth."*

This parable of the talents points out a few basic principles of being one of God's children. The point we want to focus on here is summed up in the statement: "God wants us to use the gifts he gives us for their intended purpose." The two slaves used the money for its intended purpose, the third slave did nothing. A corollary version of this parable is in Luke 19. There the master spells out what he wants done with the free gift of money: "Do business with this until I come back." This concept should not be difficult. If you take a present to a wedding, you expect the gift to be used for its intended purpose. If you have a child that is going to a local college, you might buy them a car so they can commute to class and possibly a part time job. The child may have to pay for gas and insurance, but the car is free. You expect the child to use the car for its intended purpose. We live with this concept in many various aspects of our lives.

You have been given a free gift of eternal life — are you using it for its intended purpose. Ephesians 4 tells us that to each on his given a gift of the Holy Spirit — are you using that gift for its intended purpose? God opens the door for employment — are you using that job to give witness to God and glorify Him?

Appendix B: The New Birth

What really happens at the new birth?

When I first started studying the bible, almost 55 years ago, I found out very quickly that my style of reading was introducing confusion into what I was trying to understand. What I'm about to say is not intended to be any sort of indictment against teachers in the US public schools, because they were taught this before they taught anyone else... but those raised in the US public school system were taught to read carelessly. We were taught to grasp the gist, or summarize what we are reading and move on, i.e. don't pay attention to details. Part of our brain wants to minimize the amount of information we are absorbing at any time and this compounds the problem. One of the hardest issues for law students is grasping the concept of paying attention to details, and the ones who grasp that the best, turn out to be the best lawyers.

When we read God's word, we need to pay attention to details. John 6:40 tells us: "*40 For this is the will of My Father, that everyone who beholds the Son and believes in Him will have eternal life, and I Myself will raise him up on the last day.*" John 6:40 (NASB) The word "beholds" means much more than the simplistic "I see you across the room just like you see me across the room."

"*(G2300), to look closely at. To gaze, to look with interest and for a purpose, usually indicating the careful observation of details.*" (CWSB Dictionary)

This is part of what is involved in the process of salvation, or the new birth. I've written elsewhere that "believe," verb (Strong's 4100), is derived from "faith," noun (Strong's 4102), which is derived from Strong's 3982, "persuade."

"*(G3982), πείθω peíthō; fut. peísō, aor. pass. epeísthēn, perf. pass. pépeismai, 2d perf. pépoitha. To persuade, particularly to move or affect by kind words or motives.*" (CWSB Dictio-

nary)

You will note, if you read Genesis chapter three carefully, that the serpent's temptation fits this definition of persuade perfectly. There was no force or coercion involved – part of the deception was that the serpent's description of the result of eating the forbidden fruit sounded better than anything God had said.

Faith and believe are instances of having a firm persuasion. This branch of word derivatives from persuade is in the passive voice in the Greek. Another branch of persuade is in the active voice, this is the word "trust" or "trustworthy." The active and passive voices in Greek indicate an important aspect of the word involved. The active voice means that the subject performs or experiences the action of the verb, is the cause of the action, or exists in the state of the verb. The passive voice means that the subject is acted upon. In the case of faith and believe, the subject (a person) receives the persuasion regarding what the faith/belief is in regards to. In respect to trust, that is an action initiated by the subject (a person).

"8 but to those who are selfishly ambitious and do not obey the truth, but obey unrighteousness, wrath and indignation." Romans 2:8 (NASB)

Note the use of the word "obey" twice in this verse. Both are forms of the Greek persuade (G3982). Using the meaning of persuade in this verse, it reads: "but to those who are selfishly ambitious and refuse to be persuaded to the truth, but are persuaded to unrighteousness, wrath and indignation." We can be persuaded to either righteousness (truth), or unrighteousness. Both the Holy Spirit and Satan start out on the same level playing field of persuasion. If a person chooses to be persuaded to unrighteousness, then Satan is inherently given the authority by the person for him to oppress them, to exercise power over them (Acts 10:38). If a person chooses to receive the persuasion of the Holy Spirit, then the process of the new birth starts.

Repent means a change of mind. Many think that repent means "to turn from your sins and turn to God." This is not very accurate with what Scripture describes of the new birth process – we will be detailing this as we go along.

"3340. μετανοέω metanoéō; contracted metanoō̒, fut. metanoḗsō, from metá (G3326), denoting change of place or

condition, and noéō (G3539), to exercise the mind, think, com-
prehend. To repent, change the mind, relent." (CWSB Dictio-
nary)

Now here is where many get confused because of the "popu-lar" but erroneous definition applied to repent. There are many sub-jects about which one's mind can be changed. For instance, God, sin, Bible, Jesus, judgment, resurrection, etc. Persuasion can and does touch on all these subjects and possibly more. The change of mind we are discussing is not limited to one generalized concept of salvation or whatever other descriptive wording you care to choose. Many get the individual subjects involved confused with generali-ties (think back to my comments about learning to read carelessly). See these verses regarding repent: Heb. 6:1; Acts 2:38, 3:19, 5:31, 8:22, 11: 18, 17:30-31, 19:4, 20:21, 26:19-20; Mk. 1:4, 15; Lk.. 3:3, 5:32, 13:3, 17:3, 4, 24:46-47; 2 Pet. 3:9. Repent, a change of mind, is integral and required for the new birth.

Wayne Grudem, in his book, "Free Grace Theology: 5 Ways It Diminishes The Gospel," in chapter 2, makes several statements that repent and belief take place in the heart. There are other au-thors who make similar statements, however, as I've pointed out above, there are no verses that intertwine the concepts of repent (in the mind), with belief (in the heart). Grudem also mentions in that book Hebrews 6:3, (NASB) "maturity, not laying again a foun-dation of repentance from dead works and of faith toward God," and makes a point about "from dead works," pointing out the Greek word "ἀπό" (apo) as having the meaning "from." However, the definition of "apo" can also mean "against." We have to remember that translator's opinion does enter into their work – using "against" in this instance actually goes along much better with the separa-tion identified in the bible between mind and heart, and what takes place where. See below for verses connecting belief with the heart.

"8 And He, when He comes, will convict the world
concerning sin and righteousness and judgment;" John 16:8
(NASB)

These three items, sin, righteousness, and judgment are the primary subjects that the persuasion of the Holy Spirit focuses on. I don't believe that the Holy Spirit's persuasion is limited to these, but these are the primary focus items when it comes to salvation. There is the possibility with any person that they need to have credible information, persuasion, about the truth and reliability of the bible, the existence of Jesus as a real person and the Son of God, and possibly other things.

Believing takes place in the heart, not the mind according to Scripture. I have an electronic bible app that permits me to search for combinations of words, not only within a single verse, but within a range of verses – you know the long run-on sentences that Paul uses that span as many as 10 or 12 verses??? This search capability permits me to find word associations within Paul's paragraphs, not just phrases. I searched for associations of "belie*" and "mind" within 10 verses and found nothing. (The wildcard format of "belie*" will find all forms of that – believe, belief, believed, anything beginning with "belie".) Doing a similar search on "belie*" and "heart" found these: Mk. 11:23, 16:14 Lk. 8:12, 24:5; John 14:1; Acts 8:37; Rom. 10:9-10. All this to say that the bible does not munge or mix the concepts of heart and mind when it comes to believing, the bible is not careless. 1 Corinthians 2:13, in the Greek, tells us that the Holy Spirit not only inspired or taught the words, but the expression of them (συγκρίνοντες.).

Luke 6:45 and Matthew 15:18 tell us that we speak out of what we believe in our heart. Many bible scholars think that our "conscience" is at least part of what the bible refers to when it uses the word "heart." "Heart" may involve more than just our conscience. The point to identify here is that the mind and heart have their own separate functions, but obviously have the capability of working together since persuasion is effectively the presentation of information to the mind, which then effects the belief in our heart.

The next part we need to examine is "spirit." In Luke 8:49-56, we have recorded the event where a young girl became sick, someone sent for Jesus, but before he could get there the message came that the girl had died. Jesus went anyway, threw out all but the parents in the girl's room, raised her from death, and verse 55 tells us:

"55 And her spirit returned, and she got up immediately; and He gave orders for something to be given her to eat." Luke 8:55 (NASB)

If words have any sensible meaning at all, it would be impossible for her spirit to "return" to her if it had never been there to begin with. There are some who mistakenly think that people are only body and soul, but no spirit until they are born again (or regenerate). That mistaken thought is obviously in conflict with what is actually written in Scripture (and the availability of the new birth did not start until Jesus was raised from death – John 20:22). Each of us has a spirit when we are born (conceived), which is unfortunately separated from God because of sin, requiring us to need a savior.

The word "soul" is used frequently in general conversation regarding people. When God breathed into Adam, he became a living soul (in reference to his whole being). We frequently talk about people as "body, soul, and spirit." The use of the word "soul" in the New Testament mostly refers to the entire being, not just a part of the being. There are a few references where it seems like "soul" is used instead of "heart", but they are very few.

People are comprised of mind, heart, and spirit within their physical body – in the likeness of God (from Genesis chapters one and two). So now that we have examined the pertinent parts, let's see how they are collectively effected by the new birth. I've already identified that the Holy Spirit uses persuasion to bring us to a change of mind. When that change of mind encompasses all the necessary subjects of the Holy Spirit's persuasion, the belief in the heart comes to be. I've found several dictionary descriptions of belief that include it being a "state of being." A person either believes or does not believe. A person is in one state or the other. When the change of mind exists, and the belief exists, that is when the Holy Spirit comes into the person's spirit, giving it new life, the life of the Holy Spirit. This is why the bible tells us that the Spirit is life, and gives life (Rom. 8:11; John 6:63; 2 Cor. 3:6, etc.). The time frame of all this is essentially instantaneous once the completed change of mind exists.

That still leaves the question regarding what is really going on with the popular, but erroneous, definition of repent. For this we turn to Matthew 18:3:

"3 and [Jesus] said, "Truly I say to you, unless you are converted and become like children, you will not enter the kingdom of heaven." Matthew 18:3 (NASB)

The word "converted" here is correctly translated as something that happens to the person, as opposed to something the person accomplishes. "4762. στρέφω stréphō; fut. strépsō. To turn, turn about." (CWSB Dictionary)

92

Other dictionaries include the idea of "a change of substance and direction." This change is something we cannot, by the strength of the flesh, nor the ingenuity of our minds accomplish.

This is where we can find clarification regarding the popular concept of repent. That concept is actually about the word "convert." This is something that takes place when the Holy Spirit comes into a person giving them life, eternal life. At that time, the conversion process begins. It is not an instantaneous thing. It should begin taking place during what we call discipleship, however, very few new believers are ever discipled. This turning about involves the renewal of our minds, our transformation into the image of Christ, being taught all that Jesus commanded us, getting to know what is actually written in His Word, and many other things.

So then, when the new birth takes place as described above, the converting begins. That is going to take a life time.

Appendix C: Completing the work Christ gives us

We all want to hear from Jesus, "Well done, good and faithful servant." However, I think it will be harder for us to say to Him, "I have completed the work you have given me to do." The parable of the talents gives us a stark picture of what it could be like if we do not complete the work He has given us. In that parable, two servants received a free gift of money and used it to make more money, while a third servant received a free gift of money and did nothing with it. The two were blessed and rewarded, the third was kicked out (to put it mildly). From this parable, it should seem obvious that God expects us to use the gifts given us for their intended purpose and not squandered in any manner. He has given us a free gift of eternal life, are we using it for its intended purpose? The Holy Spirit gives gifts to each and every one of his children as He wills, are you using that gift for its intended purpose?

If we are using the gift(s) given to us by God for their intended purpose, God obviously must have a reason for doing so. I seriously doubt that God just passes things around for His own exercise. To use something for its intended purpose implies that God wants something done or completed. Will we be able to say to Jesus that we have completed the work He has given us? Let's take a look at the scriptures that say something about completing things (other than the parable of the talents).

As we will see, there is more to completing something in God's economy of things than just the good word at the end. There are many present life results that are expected, and requirements that are put on us. In God's scheme of things, the end does not justify the means, as the world usually thinks. The means to God's end, or goal, must be just as holy and righteous as the end itself – it must be accomplished God's way, not the way of the flesh.

94

Repentance

"Then He began to denounce the cities in which most of His miracles were done, because they did not repent." Mt 11:20 (NASB) (done = G1096) (Definitions can be found in any lexicon or Greek dictionary.)

Repentance is one of the possible results, and requirements, of doing/using the gifts God has given us. Here, Jesus was performing miracles which was one of the prophesied indicators of the Messiah. The people did not believe that Jesus was the Messiah and repent. The meaning of "repent" is simply "to change the mind." That means that we think differently than we did before. We find evidence that "proves" that what we had been thinking is not correct, and we make the necessary corrections.

Walk by faith, not by sight

"But the synagogue official, indignant because Jesus had healed on the Sabbath, began saying to the crowd in response, "There are six days in which work should be done; so come during them and get healed, and not on the Sabbath day." " Lu. 13:14 (NASB) (work = G2038, done = G4160)

Legalism in any form will impede the work God wants done. Legalism is a set of man-made rules and regulations that people impose so that they can feel like they are the ones in control of things instead of God. Healing and doing things on the Sabbath was one of the things that the legalistic Jewish leadership became most perturbed about. The real problem was that most of the legalistic rules they imposed on themselves and others were not well founded in the Mosaic Law. God had given the Ten Commandments and some rules about making sacrifices and Holy Days throughout the calendar year, but the religious leaders took that to an extreme and had over 600 rules they had to abide by. Most of those rules went way beyond anything God had stated. What kind of a God would He be if He refuses to give someone the new birth because it is Sunday? That is essentially what this religious official was intimating. "Come back on a work day to get saved." A very incomplete spiritual concept that is totally lacking in love. Legalism is nothing more or less than walking by sight and not be faith. We can never be saved by works or rules and regulations – only by faith.

Righteous acts expose sin in others

"If I had not done among them the works which no one else did, they would not have sin; but now they have both seen and hated Me and My Father as well." John 15:24 (NASB) (done = G4160, works = G2041)

When we execute on something that is holy and righteous, we create an environment which is an extreme contrast between the sinful ways of the world and the ways of God. This contrast very simply exposes sin in people's lives. They then have the choice of either accepting the exposure of their sin and doing something about it (repenting and finding salvation in Jesus) or rejecting it. The complaint Jesus had against the people who saw and/or experienced the miracles (works) that Jesus did, was that they refused to accept the fact that the kingdom of God had come among them in the form of the son of God, and thereby rejected both Jesus and God the Father. (See John 14: 7, 9 that whoever saw Jesus has seen the Father.) When people see a Christian doing something holy and righteous, it is for them like seeing Jesus, and His presence in us exposes their sin. When we are doing something unrighteous, and people know we are Christians, we ... (you finish the thought).

Press on to completion - Participate

"So we urged Titus that as he had previously made a beginning, so he would also complete in you this gracious work as well." 2Co 8:6 (NASB) (complete = G2005, gracious work = G5485)

Here we read that Paul is urging Titus to continue on with the work Titus had begun in the Corinthian believers. Exactly what the specific details of that work were, we are not told. But by stating this, Paul is also implying that the Corinthian believers should cooperate with Titus in achieving the completion of whatever it was. In the Hebrew mind back in Bible times, most times when something is NOT said, it is just as important as what IS said. In other words, we need to pay serious attention to the implications, or inference, of what IS said. So, if Titus is to complete something, the rhetorical inference is that the Corinthian believers should be cooperating (or participating) with Titus.

This principle of participating with God in our growth and relationship to Him is something that many believers overlook to their own detriment. Picture a small baby child who refuses to eat (participate in its own growth and development). Obviously if the parents don't do something, the child would die of starvation. The same idea applies to our own spiritual growth. We have to participate in reading the bible, fellowship with other believers, praying, get involved in biblical oriented education [Sunday School and more], discipleship, sharing Jesus with others, etc., otherwise we become stagnant. Jesus stated that if we are not for Him, we are against Him. When we stop growing spiritually, we start a reverse process of shutting Jesus out of our lives. Not a good situation.

Participate

"in view of your participation in the gospel from the first day until now. For I am confident of this very thing, that He who began a good work in you will perfect it until the day of Christ Jesus." Php. 1:5, 6 (NASB) (work = G2041, perfect = G2005)

Paul, writing to the Philippians, is telling them that God has started something in them, and God can and will bring it to completion or perfection. That might just take a whole life time, but God will do it. This is something that we cannot accomplish in our own strength of our flesh. We must watch and see (usually in hindsight) that God is transforming our minds and strengthening our faith in Him. Here again, we see that Paul is identifying the "participation" of the Philippians as an ongoing part of the work God is accomplishing in them.

Fulfill the need in others

"because he came close to death for the work of Christ, risking his life to complete what was deficient in your service to me." Php. 2:30 (NASB) (work = G2041, complete = G378)

"But I have received everything in full and have an abundance; I am amply supplied, having received from Epaphroditus what you have sent, a fragrant aroma, an acceptable sacrifice, well-pleasing to God." Php. 4:18 (NASB)

Paul is talking about Epaphroditus who had come from Philippi to visit Paul in prison and help take care of Paul's needs. There were things which the Philippians had started with Paul and were not immediately able to complete, so Epaphroditus came to finish things. The point here is that whatever Paul's needs were that had not yet been met, God provided someone to fill the gap. God wants things taken care of completely. (See discussion below on Phil. 2:12-13.)

Build on God's foundation

"Therefore leaving the elementary teaching about the Christ, let us press on to maturity, not laying again a foundation of repentance from dead works and of faith toward God," Heb. 6:1 (NASB) (maturity = G5047, works = G2041)

Maturity is the completion of the process of growing up. Spiritually, I'm somewhat suspicious that it really takes more than a lifetime from our temporal human perspective. If God is infinite (as He really is), then we might just be continuing our growth throughout eternity. The descriptor used with "works" in this statement is "dead." Dead could also mean lifeless, most likely in this usage it means the things we do prior to finding salvation in Jesus. Before salvation, we are "dead" meaning separated from God. Just as a corpse cannot accomplish anything beyond decaying (getting worse), before we find salvation, we cannot of our own works or strength do anything to bring about a relation to God for eternal life. The point the writer is making is that we need to leave behind all the ways and means of the world system we have been saved out of, and find the spiritual growth and maturity that God wants us to have while we are here on Earth.

Endurance

"And let endurance have its perfect result, so that you may be perfect and complete, lacking in nothing." Jas. 1:4 (NASB) (perfect = G5046, complete = G3648)

Endurance is an essential requirement for continued participation in the work God wants to accomplish in you. We can never achieve anything completely if we quit part way through. James identifies that God wants us to be lacking in nothing. That is the perfect (completed) result God is striving for in us. God has given us eternal life: His word so we can know him intimately, the Holy Spirit in power so we can live the life He wants of us, and a gift of the Spirit so we know what He wants us to be doing as He works

His perfection in us. He has given us everything we need, we just need to let Him work and be willing participants toward His goals in our life.

Hearing requires obedience

"But one who looks intently at the perfect law, the law of liberty, and abides by it, not having become a forgetful hearer but an effectual doer, this man will be blessed in what he does." Jas 1:25 (NASB) (perfect = G5046, doer = G4163, does = G4162)

James is telling us that we need to obey what we hear from God and His word, to take those words and make them actions in our life. God tells us several times in His word that we need to pay attention to every one of His words, we do not have any options to add to His word, nor to omit any of His word (Deut. 4:2, 18:18-20; Prov. 30.6; Jer. 26:2; Rev. 22:18-19). God wants us to pay attention to everything He says and wants to accomplish in us.

Our obedience perfects our faith

"You see that faith was working with his works, and as a result of the works, faith was perfected;" Jas 2:22 (NASB) (working = G4903, works = G2041, perfected = G5048)

James brings us to the point that the faith we live by is perfected, brought to completion, through the things and activities we participate in that are directed by God.

Jesus really will reward us

"Behold, I am coming quickly, and My reward is with Me, to render to every man according to what he has done." Re 22:12 (NASB) (what he has done = G2041)

There is a reward for what we do while we are here on Earth. The parable of the talents identifies the two servants who completed their tasks were told the desirous "Well done good and faithful servant. Enter into the joy of your master." Hearing that will depend on our obedience and participation in God's work in us to bring us to completion, perfection, not lacking anything.

There is effort involved after we find salvation in Jesus:

"So then, my beloved, just as you have always obeyed, not as in my presence only, but now much more in my absence, work out your salvation with fear and trembling; for it is God who is at work in you, both to will and to work for His good pleasure." Php. 2:12-13 (NASB)

The two English words, "work out" come from one word in the Greek. It simply means "to accomplish something successfully and with thoroughness." The fear and trembling have the typical meaning we commonly think of. The work involved takes place in two arenas – God is at work, and the second work is what is taking place in us (our participation) looking forward to God's pleasure, which is our will. We want God to be pleased with us.

The word "will" is one of the most misunderstood words in theology. Many versions of the bible will frequently use the word "desire" instead of "will." Too many Christians seem to use the word "will" as though it means something very adamant, very much set in concrete. That is not what it means. The common idea is an extreme that none of the half-dozen or so dictionaries/Lexicons I've examined indicate. We need to apply a "softer" sense of the meaning of the word "will." Some of the words used to define "will" are "prefer," "desire," "intend." None of those words are anywhere near as extreme, hard, and unchangeable as most people think of the word "will." In the Greek, there are two words (with a few minor variations of form to indicate case, gender, voice, etc.) that are translated as "will." These are (transliterated) "thelw" and "boulomai." Thelw is used at least 200 times in the New Testament, bouloumai is only used about 34 times. Bouloumai is a stronger form of "will," however, neither word contains within its meaning any absolute requirement of completion. People use the term "will" too frequently meaning (in their own minds only) something that is concrete, absolute, unchangeable, never to be altered – but the words do not support their misunderstanding.

Our will, our intent, our preference, our desire, is to be pleasing to God – or at least it should be. If we really want to hear Him say, "Well done good and faithful servant," we must have a desire, a very deep seated desire, an endurance, a growing and deepening faith, a repentant mind, a believing heart, a willingness to participate in what God is doing in our lives, be willing to fill the gap in some other Christians life whom God is also working in and allow another to work in our life, be obedient, put forth whatever effort is involved. Without those characteristics at work in our lives, it should be obvious, the completion or perfection God wants in us might not take place.

"14 But thanks be to God, who always leads us in triumph in Christ, and manifests through us the sweet aroma of the knowledge of Him in every place. 15 For we are a fragrance of Christ to God among those who are being saved and among those who are perishing; 16 to the one an aroma from death to death, to the other an aroma from life to life. And who is adequate for these things?" 2 Corinthians 2:14-16 (NASB)

If proper inference is applied here, the lack of knowledge of Him will not produce a "sweet aroma," and the aroma we do produce will be "death to death" instead of "life to life." Our salvation presents the opportunity for those currently in "death" to find life. Yes, there are difficulties we must face and overcome in order for God's perfection or completion to be worked out in us. It is most definitely worth the effort and risk. God wants to work in us, and He requires us to "work" with Him, participate with Him in whatever way He leads us. He is the one who can see the end from the beginning, not us. Those who think that God is the only one responsible for "getting us to heaven" have failed to read what is actually written. There really are requirements on us to participate, to work along with God in getting things completed.

Acts 10:38 tells us that oppression comes from the devil. Oppression means "to exercise power over another." To think that God somehow "forces" or "coerces" us into being obedient is simply blasphemy (attributing to God something that really is evil). We need to be willing participants in what God wants to do in our life. Just as we do not have any instruction or permission from God to leave out anything in His word, neither do we have any say in the matter of what takes place so that our faith can be perfected. We cannot "order Him around." We must willingly work with God at our side, and the strength of the Holy Spirit within us to see it happen.

Appendix D: forgive

The most basic concept underlying forgiveness is the shed blood of Christ on the cross and his resurrection from the grave. Without the shedding of blood there is no forgiveness of sins. This concept will not be repeated within this article so that we can concentrate on the application of the meaning of forgive to our lives. Please keep this concept in mind as the basis for the following discussion of forgive.

"11 For the life of the flesh is in the blood, and I have given it for you on the altar to make atonement for your souls, for it is the blood that makes atonement by the life." Leviticus 17:11 (ESV)

"22 And according to the Law, one may almost say, all things are cleansed with blood, and without shedding of blood there is no forgiveness." Hebrews 9:22 (NASB)

The most frequently used word in the Greek that is translated "forgive," really means "to send away." (Watch the 'humor' here...) So, if you say to God: "Forgive me," could you actually be asking God to send you away? Enter the problem of most of us being taught to read carelessly (and communicate in general in a careless manner). We should really be asking God: "Forgive me of my sins," meaning to send our sins away (not us). Fortunately, God understands us better than we understand ourselves...

The word most frequently translated "forgive" has two forms which are very similar in meaning: "aphiemi" (G0863) means "to send away," and "aphesis" (G0859) means "dismissal, release." The other word that is sometimes translated "forgive" is "charizomai" (G5483) whose root is "charis" (G5485) which means "grace, kindness." Picture it this way: when you ask God to forgive you of your sins, you are asking for His kindness and grace to send your sins away. If you are forgiving someone of the sins committed against you, you are sending those sins away from yourself. Here is where it has been most difficult for people to forgive others for the crimes committed. We think we are send those sins away from that other person, when in reality we are only sending them away from ourselves.

When someone else commits a sin against you, they are still going to be responsible to God for each and every sin they commit, no matter to who, or what it might be. When we send those sins away from ourselves, we are removing ourselves from the situation of being Judge and Juror for that person and allowing God to be the only Judge and Juror as He stated in Deuteronomy 32:35, and Romans 12:19, "Vengeance is mine, I will repay," and "Do not take revenge..." God's final judgment of being committed to the Lake of Fire for eternity is much harsher than anything we could impose. The one needing to do the forgiving (sending sins away from themselves) needs to realize that if the other person were punished according to what we could come up with, we would be letting them off easy. God is not "easy" when it comes to punishing sin. When we hold onto the sins committed against us by another, we are in a state of unforgiveness, which is an unforgivable sin, which means we bear the burden of punishment for holding onto those sins committed against us. I have yet to find a sensible rationale for getting the same punishment as the offender against us, for holding on to those sins. In the case where a young girl is sexually abused by her father, she can only send the sins she bears away from herself because she does not have spiritual authority over her father to send his sins away.

In Matthew 8 and Luke 7 the incident is recorded where a centurion requests healing from Jesus for his servant who is paralyzed and severely tormented. Jesus intended to go to the centurion's house, but the centurion made an interesting statement about authority. He was under authority and his soldiers and servants were under his authority, and the healing and deliverance requested from Jesus could be spoken and be just as effective as Jesus going there. This concept of being under authority cannot be ignored. Each of us has authority over ourselves and those under us (children, spouse), but we do not have authority over those "above" us in the authority structure. A servant does not have authority over the master. So, when we are traumatized in whatever way from someone in higher authority, we do not have authority to cast their sins away from them – we can only cast any from ourselves.

When sins are sent away, Psalms 103:12 comes into play: "As far as the east is from the west, So far has He removed our transgressions from us." Here's the picture, please read this carefully. When we sin, we are responsible for that sin. Before people existed, God had already established the required punishment of death (separation from God) for sin (no matter how "slight" or "heinous"). God never "pardons" sin the way we think of "pardon" in our US court and presidential systems, because under these systems the sin still exists, just the immediate punishment is taken away. With God, sin is always punished. If we have sin, we must bear the burden of punishment. If our sins are sent away from ourselves, then those sins are no longer with us and since we then have no sin, we have no burden of judgment to bear for those sins. In other words, the judgment for sin falls where the sin resides. When God sends our sins away from us, they are as far from Him as they are from us. If you wish, you could consider that when sins are sent away, they are effectively annihilated, which is how the sin is punished (but not us).

This gives us better understanding of part of the issue people usually refer to as "the age of accountability" and what I've written about that subject previously. What I wrote is not wrong, just has a missing piece that I've just identified. Job is the basic example of the situation. Job offered sacrifices every day on behalf of his children in case they might have sinned. The sacrifices offered by Job paid the penalty for any sins of the children. If the head of an unbelieving family desires for the child of the family to go to heaven in the event of death, there is no hope. The father, mother, and child do not believe, are all sinners, and have no hope unless they find salvation in Jesus. The concept of "all things work together for good" only applies to those who love God and are called accordance to His purpose – unbelievers do not love God and are not called according to His purpose. In the early AD400's a bishop in Britain named Plagius picked up on a Gnostic heresy from the late AD100's that stated all people are born sinless. Plagius did this because of all the wars and raids going on in Britain at the time, and parents were concerned about the children who were being killed in these raids. This situation was one of the primary motivators for the false concept of "Age of Accountability." David identifies in Psalm 51 that he was conceived in sin – i.e. we are born a sinner, separated from God and have no hope except in Jesus, if we believe on Him.

In a believing family, the father, the spiritual head of the family can exercise something similar to what Job did.

"14 For the unbelieving husband is sanctified through his wife, and the unbelieving wife is sanctified through her believing husband; for otherwise your children are unclean, but now they are holy." 1 Corinthians 7:14 (NASB)

"31 They said, "Believe in the Lord Jesus, and you will be saved, you and your household."" Acts 16:31 (NASB)

I have read every commentary I have in my bible app (17) and several others online, and found the same thing in each and every one of them. The commentaries will define the words "holy" and "sanctified" a certain way for uses other than 1 Cor.7:14 as describing the truly born-again saint, but here they twist their definition so that they can rationalize away the true meaning of the word. They usually say something to the effect of the child has a better opportunity to find salvation (which has some truth to it). In basic reading fundamentals, there is a rule called "The Rule of Consistency." Every one of those commentaries violate that rule. They are inconsistent and different in their definition of "holy" and "sanctified" just for this verse. The question they avoid is identified in Acts 6:31 – how could the head of the house be deemed saved "and your household" if the head of the house cannot impart his own holiness and sanctification from God to the members of his family? This destroys the whole concept of spiritual covering. Of what use could it possibly be then for there to be a spiritual head of the family? If the commentaries are correct in their twisted definition of holy and sanctified for just this verse, then the statement in Acts 16:31 is a lie. The real problem with the position the commentaries take is that the same Holy Spirit who inspired the words in both verses, and how to express them (1 Cor. 2:13 in the Greek). I have yet to discover any real evidence that the Holy Spirit is suffering from multiple personality disorder or schizophrenia. God does not mean one thing in one place and something different in another place when using the same words.

All that to come to the point that the head of the family can do the similar thing that Job did. Every day the head of the family can intercede for each child.

"23 If you forgive the sins of any, their sins have been forgiven them; if you retain the sins of any, they have been retained." John 20:23 (NASB)

Along with the whole household being saved (Acts 16:31), the example of Job, and the sanctification from the believing partner in marriage, this verse wraps up the whole picture. The believing head of the family can apply the forgiveness of sin (the sending away of sin) for the children.

To put all these pieces together lets the picture look like this: The most frequently used word in the Greek for "forgive" simply means "to send away." The next most used word in the Greek that is sometimes translated "forgive" is based on "charis" which means "grace or kindness." So, when we ask God to forgive us of our sins, we are asking Him to extend his grace and kindness to us and send our sins away. We then have no sin for which we must bear the burden of punishment. We must send away from ourselves any sins committed against us by another, again, so that there are no sins for which we must bear the burden of punishment. If we send them away, they are sent away; if we hold on to them, we will bear the burden of punishment for them. The born-again head of the family can do a "Job stunt" for the children of the family, thereby extending the sending away of sins that might have been committed by the children. God is not schizophrenic about the meanings of words; if they mean "holy" and "sanctified" everywhere else, they mean the same thing when it comes to the description of the possibly unbelieving marriage partner and children.

Forgive means to send the sins away.

Any sin you keep in your heart will block all answers to prayer. Any sin you hang on to will require judgment.

GET RID OF THEM!